# The Outrageous Idea of Christian Scholarship

GEORGE M. MARSDEN

*New York   Oxford*

OXFORD UNIVERSITY PRESS

*1997*

Oxford University Press

Oxford   New York
Athens   Auckland   Bangkok   Bogotá   Bombay
Buenos Aires   Calcutta   Cape Town   Dar es Salaam
Delhi   Florence   Hong Kong   Istanbul   Karachi
Kuala Lumpur   Madras   Madrid   Melbourne
Mexico City   Nairobi   Paris   Singapore
Taipei   Tokyo   Toronto
and associated companies in
Berlin   Ibadan

Published by Oxford University Press, Inc.
198 Madison Avenue, New York, New York 10016

Oxford is a registered trademark of Oxford University Press

Library of Congress Cataloging-in-Publication Data
Marsden, George M., 1939–
The outrageous idea of Christian scholarship / George M. Marsden.
p.   cm.   Includes bibliographical references and index.
ISBN 0-19-510565-6
1. Education (Christian theology).
2. Education, Higher—Aims and objectives—United States.
I. Title.
BT738.17.M37   1996   377—dc20   96-22280

1   3   5   7   9   8   6   4   2

Printed in the United States of America
on acid-free paper

In Memory of

George A. Rawlyk

1935–1995

*He showed us not only how to be a Christian scholar,*

*but also how to live like one.*

# Preface

In *The Soul of the American University: From Protestant Establishment to Established Nonbelief* (Oxford Univ. Press, 1994), I explored how and why American university culture, which was constructed largely by Protestants, has come to provide so little encouragement for academically rigorous perspectives explicitly shaped by Christian or other religious faith. One theme of *The Soul of the American University* is that the century-long process of dismantling the old Protestant establishment was, among other things, an understandable way of addressing problems of equity in an increasingly pluralistic society. However, as I argued in a "Concluding Unscientific Postscript," the dominant university culture has overcorrected to the point that expressions of religious perspectives are liable to be considered inappropriate or offensive.

As might be expected, that "Postscript," in which I stepped into a more prescriptive role, has drawn the attention of critics. In particular, they have asked what I had in mind by "Christian scholarship," an idea that I claimed had relevance to much of academic life. Many people find this idea strange unless it refers only to theology or to study *about* religious topics. Outside of that, they have no idea what it might mean. Reviewers have also raised a number of helpful questions about the appropriateness of introducing explicitly faith-informed perspectives into mainstream academia.

I am grateful to all those who have responded to my proposal and for the present opportunity to explain more fully what I have in mind. I am particularly grateful to those who have spoken out frankly and raised some hard questions. I appreciate the good spirit of the debate and I hope I have answered their questions, at the least, fairly. Even though I use some of their comments as points of departure, the goal of this volume is not primarily to respond to critics. Rather, the goal is to take a step toward clarifying what the ancient enterprise of relating faith and learning might mean in the academy today.

I also want to thank my many friends who have helped me with this volume. These include many friendly respondents at numerous lectures, conferences, and symposia. Especially, however, I want to thank those friends who took the time from extremely busy schedules to read and comment on the entire manuscript. These include Michael Beaty, Paul Kemeny, Mark Noll, James Turner, and John Van Engen. Lucie also gave me some good advice and her love and good humor have once again been more valuable than I can possibly express.

Cynthia Read again has gone beyond the duties of a senior editor in providing needed stylistic editing. I am grateful also to Stephanie Sakson for copyediting and to Karin Commeret for proofreading.

I am continually grateful to the McAnaney family for the Francis A. McAnaney Chair, which has been a source of ongoing support for this work. I am also grateful to the administration of the University of Notre Dame and to many congenial colleagues and graduate students.

Parts of this material were presented as the 1995 Walter Pope Binns Lectures at William Jewell College and I am grateful to my hosts there for their hospitality and support. Chapter 3, "Christian Scholarship and the Rules of the Academic Game," originated as a paper presented at a conference on advocacy and scholarship sponsored by the Institute for the Study of American Evangelicalism. I am grateful for the comments I received at that time and for permission to publish a version of the argument here. The original together with other papers from that conference are being published as *Religious Advocacy and the Writing of American History* (Grand Rapids: William B. Eerdmans, 1997). That volume provides some valuable discussion of the broader issue of advocacy, especially in relation to religious faith.

*March 1996*                                                                 G. M.

# Contents

The Outrageous Idea of Christian Scholarship

# Introduction

Contemporary university culture is hollow at its core. Not only does it lack a spiritual center, but it is also without any real alternative. Although many of the most prominent academics are preoccupied with politics, they are unable to produce a compelling basis for preferring one set of principles over another. On the contrary, while they tend to be dogmatic moralists, many also espouse theories that would undermine not only traditional moral norms, but their own as well. Others, probably most academics, do not even try to deal with first principles. Knowledge today is oriented increasingly toward the practical; at the same time, in most fields the vast increases in information render our expertise more fragmentary and detached from the larger issues of life. Although the university research ideal apparently works well enough in the sciences and technology, it is not at all clear why the same principles should be normative for the study of human society and behavior. Even the liberal arts are havens for fads that often obscure what was originally attractive about their subjects. "Wisdom" is hardly a term one thinks of in connection with such studies, nor with our system of higher education generally.

The proposal set forth in this volume will not solve all these problems, but it will help many people draw on some rich and largely untapped resources in addressing them. The proposal is that mainstream American higher education should be more open to explicit discussion of the relationship of religious faith to learning. Scholars who have religious faith should be reflecting on the intellectual implications of that faith and bringing those reflections into the mainstream of intellectual life. Although scholars of no faith or of other faiths may strongly disagree on the particular issues involved, all should participate on equal terms in academic dialogue.

The incoherence of mainstream higher education prompts us to reexamine the assumptions on which modern education has been built and to consider constructive alternatives. Particularly, the current state of academia invites the reexamination of the assumption, popular through much of this century, that our educational system would be better off if it were free from the heritages of ancient religious learning.

In challenging this assumption I am not primarily concerned with the *fields* of theology or religious studies which of course still have their place among our hundreds of isolated academic enterprises. Rather I am advocating the opening of the academic mainstream to scholarship that relates one's belief in God to what else one thinks about. Keeping within our intellectual horizons a being who is great enough to create us and the universe, after all, ought to change our perspectives on quite a number of things. One might expect it to have a bearing on some of the most sharply debated issues in academia today: How can we find a basis for our most cherished moral judgments? Is power the only means to decide what counts as "virtue"? How can we affirm a pluralism that genuinely accepts others, without lapsing into relativism? Can we know anything about reality that goes beyond our own socially determined constructions? Are there any essential traits in the human character? Is there any alternative to the fragmentation of the disciplines? What should be the relationships among research, teaching, and other service? What is the point of an academic career?[1]

Scholars whose intellectual lives are informed by their faith will give many different and sometimes mutually exclusive answers to these questions. Yet with God in the picture these issues, which have brought modern intellectual life to its current dysfunctional impasse, can be viewed in fresh and promising ways. In light of this potential, why, in a culture in which many academics profess to believe in God, do so few reflect on the academic implications of that belief?

Unquestionably one of the main reasons so few reflect on the implications of faith for learning is that they have been formed by an academic culture in which such reflection is discouraged. While most academics simply have not thought much about the issue, at least a vocal minority react with complete puzzlement or even vehement opposition to the idea of introducing religious perspectives into the academic mainstream. On the face of it, such reactions seem at odds with other current academic attitudes. Religious commitments, after all, are basic to the identities and social location of many if not most human beings, and academics routinely recognize such factors as having intellectual significance. Religious beliefs, moreover, typically involve affirmations about reality and values that are far more specific and far-ranging than beliefs inherent to gender, race, ethnicity, or class. Nonetheless it is not unusual for otherwise judicious scholars to dismiss the idea of the relevance of religious perspectives to respectable scholarship as absurd.

## THE OUTRAGEOUS IDEA

When *The Chronicle of Higher Education* reported on proposals such as that just stated, a leading American intellectual historian responded that "... the notion that scholars' personal beliefs are compatible with their academic interests is 'loony' and reflects 'a self-indulgent professoriate.'" He added (in the reporter's words) that "an important distinction must be made between supernatural and non-supernatural ideas. Gender and race are empirical constructs: one's faith is not."[2]

Such comments reflect widespread, even if far from universal, opinion. Almost any public discussion of this issue will elicit similarly strong reactions from some thoughtful people. It is very common, for instance, for academics to dismiss religion as simply non-empirical and therefore worthy of no serious consideration. One letter to the *Chronicle* claimed that professors who are religious believers refuse to rigorously examine their own religious beliefs. "If they'd research even the religious philosophies they've accepted, then they could actually call themselves 'scholars.' But they won't." Another academic wrote that "those professors who wish to present their religious views in the classroom would do well to state frankly: 'Many of my beliefs respecting supernatural phenomena are beyond what we have accepted as standards for scholarly proof in modern universities.'" Another went even further, asserting that matters of religion are "by definition not amenable to logic."[3]

5

While science is often the authority cited in dismissing religious perspectives, politics lends fervor to the cause. The historian who remarked that the idea of introducing Christian perspectives was "loony" added that "the conservative Christians clamoring loudest to be heard have a poor record of accommodating the voices of women and blacks."[4] This comment points to a real weakness in many efforts by Christians to strengthen their place in the public sphere. Critics are quick to note that no group has a history of more privilege, and even among academics today one can find a substantial number of professing Christians; it therefore seems disingenuous for Christians to claim to be a victimized group of outsiders. Even though there may be cases of discrimination, such critics point out, many other groups have suffered much more, often at the hands of Christians. Finally, it is said that the respect accorded to a number of avowedly Christian scholars proves that there is no general anti-religious discrimination in the academy.

I want to emphasize that this book is not about victimization or personal discrimination against Christians. Anti-religious prejudice or perceived prejudice is sometimes a factor, but the main issue is a different one. It is the puzzling phenomenon that, among so many academics who are professing Christians, all but a tiny minority keep quiet about the intellectual implications of their faith.[5] Why are there in mainstream academia almost no identifiable Christian schools of thought to compare with various Marxist, feminist, gay, post-modern, African-American, conservative, or liberal schools of thought? If one compares, for example, the number of Marxists in America with the number of Christians, the disparity in their visibility in mainstream academia is truly remarkable. What is it about the dominant academic culture that teaches people they must suppress reflection on the intellectual implications of their faith?

Nowhere is this phenomenon more strikingly apparent than in the field of religious studies, which is also sharply divided over these issues. Teachers of religion in seminaries and in many church-related colleges are often deeply committed to their faith, as are some at secular colleges and universities. Over the past few decades, however, they have been confronted with a dominant university culture in which explicit religious perspectives, or at least explicit Christian perspectives, are increasingly considered unscientific and unprofessional. In 1993 I encountered that divided opinion directly when I had the privilege of addressing a plenary session of the American

Academy of Religion. My topic, "Religious Commitment in the Academy," created quite a stir and even received considerable news coverage. One comment, reported in the *New York Times,* encapsulated particularly well the reason why my views were controversial. John C. Green, a political scientist, observed that

> If a professor talks about studying something from a Marxist point of view, others might disagree but not dismiss the notion. But if a professor proposed to study something from a Catholic or Protestant point of view, it would be treated like proposing something from a Martian point of view.[6]

Green's remarks zeroed in on the crucial issue. Even though many academics are religious, they would consider it outrageous to speak of the relationship of their faith to their scholarship. That is true not only in religious studies, but also in almost every discipline, no matter how relevant religious beliefs might potentially be to academic interpretation.

The fact is that, no matter what the subject, our dominant academic culture trains scholars to keep quiet about their faith as the price of full acceptance in that community. True, there are some senior scholars—perhaps a growing number—who have successfully defied the convention. By and large, however, the process of acculturation teaches those entering the profession that concerns about faith are an intrusion that will meet with deep resentment from at least a minority of their colleagues and superiors. Added to this is the alleged dogma of "separation of church and state" which, while often misunderstood, indeed does raise some delicate issues. Even at church-related schools, however, the pervasive reach of the dominant academic culture is evident among the many professors who insist that it is inappropriate to relate their Christianity to their scholarship.

Separation of faith and learning is widely taken for granted in our culture. An observer from another era, however, would find it puzzling that so many Christian academics seem to accept it without question. Most of these same academics, one would suppose, would affirm that Christianity should not be merely a Sunday church activity, but should relate to everyday life. Because they are educators, they would doubtless also affirm that education is one of the crucial dimensions of everyday life. Nonetheless, they accept the conclusion (more of a premise in most of academic culture) that Christian perspectives are inappropriate to the best scholarship.

THEMES, PERSPECTIVES, AND GOALS

It was this puzzle that sent me on an historical quest to understand how American university culture came to take for granted its current stance regarding religious perspectives. *The Soul of the American University: From Protestant Establishment to Established Nonbelief* explores that theme. This book builds on that historical analysis, which I review in the first chapter. Chapter Two attempts to answer some common arguments for minimizing faith-informed perspectives. The main point of the present volume, however, is to provide some positive guidelines as to what I have in mind when I urge that Christian perspectives and the perspectives of other religious groups be accepted as legitimate in the mainstream academy.

This book is addressed to two audiences. First it is for mainstream university scholars who have been skeptical about the idea of taking religious faith seriously as a factor in intellectual life. Some of them have reacted with passion when I have put forward this proposal in the past. Others have listened politely, but they honestly cannot understand what it means when I say that Christian or other religious outlooks should be recognized among the serious perspectives in the academic mainstream.

The second audience is Christians and other religious people, especially scholars, who recognize that there might be something like religiously informed scholarship, but are not clear as to what it amounts to. While we have some good examples of religious scholarship today, these are not often well known and there is much additional work to be done. Many academics who are religious simply have not reflected much on the relationship of their religion to their intellectual life.

Among those scholars who are religious I am specifically addressing Christians, since that is my own faith. There are not simply "religious" views of various subjects. There are only the views of particular religions, so it makes most sense to talk about my own. Nevertheless, the viewpoints of the major monotheistic religions overlap at many points and the point of view of one may have much in common with the concerns of others.

On specific issues, I speak from a particular branch of Christendom, shaped by confessional Protestantism in the Augustinian and more recent Reformed tradition. That tradition is one of several with a distinguished intellectual heritage. Augustinians have characteristically emphasized the principle that faith precedes and conditions understanding. *Credo ut intelligam*. The characteristic insights growing out of this heritage are part of a mainstream of almost two millennia of discussion, and Christians from many other heritages and persons from other religious traditions may find them illuminating as well. Those who recognize the pretheoretical conditions of knowledge should be especially open to the constructive insights of this heritage.

It must be confessed, however, that Christians of all heritages have often oversimplified the question of the relationship of faith to learning, thus inviting some of the current confusion as to what Christian scholarship might mean. Many people assume, for instance, that relating Christianity to scholarship must involve practices like interpreting history in terms of God's particular providences, celebrating the triumphs of the spiritual, favoring hagiography over criticism with respect to one's own tradition, or identifying when the Holy Spirit is or is not shaping events. When I try to explain that this is not what I have in mind, I almost invariably get questions something like this: "Outside of theology itself, do Christian perspectives really make much difference in scholarship? After all, there is no Christian mathematics or no distinctly Christian way of measuring chemical reactions. So what are we talking about? Isn't the best Christian scholarship simply to be the best scholar one can be? Aren't we all looking for the truth and so shouldn't we just use the best means to find it?" Most often such questions come from people who have had some religious schooling that was superficial and triumphalist. Their early experience with such teachings has steeled their resolve to limit scholarship to what they considered to be the strictly professional.

One of the goals of this book, then, is to explain how, without resort to dogmatism or heavy-handed moralizing, Christian faith can be of great relevance to contemporary scholarship of the highest standards. A subtheme is that such scholarship is an alternative not only to the hollow secularism that dominates mainstream academia but also to the simplistic "fundamentalisms" that present themselves as the only alternatives.

The answers to the questions of relating Christian faith to contemporary scholarship are not simple. Perhaps most difficult are the questions about introducing the affirmations of a particular religious faith into a pluralistic setting. Many people find that prospect inherently offensive. How might it be done without violating legitimate concerns to maintain peace and mutual respect in a pluralistic environment?

Sometimes people simply object to any idea of scholarship as "Christian," as expressing religious prejudice because it not only distinguishes Christian views from those of other religious faiths but also suggests that the Christian ones are superior. This is something of a red herring; everyone believes his or her views to be superior to alternative views. Perhaps, if we lived at a time when Christian views were legally or virtually established and other views were excluded, such objections would carry some force. In our time, though, that is hardly the issue. As long as we are talking about *voluntary* religious expressions, a Christian point of view is no more exclusive of other views or of other faiths than any other point of view. Even those who profess to be relativists treat other viewpoints as inferior to their relativism and try to convince others of their viewpoint. Indeed sometimes they are rather dogmatic.

In this connection I need to emphasize, as I have in my historical writing, that I see formal or informal religious establishments by the state as characteristically sources of complacency and injustice. I am emphatically not proposing a return to a "golden age" when there was a Christian establishment in the academic mainstream. Rather, whatever I propose by way of making a place for Christian scholars should apply, *mutatis mutandis,* to Jews, Muslims, Buddhists, Hindus, and persons of other religious faiths or of no formal faith.

In fact, in some pluralistic settings it may be best not usually to use "Christian," "Jewish," "Islamic," or so forth as an adjective in reference to one's scholarship. "Faith-informed scholarship" might be preferable. It is both more modest and less likely to accentuate differences among faiths. So long as one does not lose sight of the relevant particularities of one's own faith, that seems to me a sensible concession. Broadly understood, faith in something or other informs all scholarship.[7] So the phrase "faith-informed" emphasizes that belief systems built around organized religious faiths should in principle have equal standing with other worldviews.

Recognition of the necessity and value of a plurality of voices in the academic mainstream means that religious scholars must accommodate their messages to the legitimate demands of a pluralistic setting. If they wish to participate in such a setting (and some may not), they need to respect some conventions that make it possible for people to communicate and to get along when they differ as to first principles.

These observations will immediately raise objections from some who are deeply religious. Am I not saying in effect that they will have to compromise their faith? As Christians are likely to put it, are we not serving two masters if we attempt to be faithful to our faith community and try also to gain a hearing among a wider academic audience? Should Christian scholars expect or desire to be fully accepted in mainstream academia, where their basic commitments will often be regarded as foolishness? Does playing by the rules of the dominant academic community inevitably compromise one's faith?

Such difficult questions are at the heart of this volume. How does the religiously commmited scholar accommodate to the demands of the mainstream academic profession without compromising her faith? Especially important are the issues concerning what kinds of differences religious scholarship might make when addressed to the mainstream academy and, more particularly, what differences Christian theological perspectives might make.

Finally, what are the institutional implications? What standing should institutions that support or encourage Christian or other religious scholarship have in the academic mainstream? As the historical review in the first chapter suggests, for the past century academic prestige has been closely correlated with the jettisoning of institutional religious heritages. In the United States many of the most distinguished colleges and universities have had close relationships to Protestant churches, but today none of these leading schools unambiguously promotes Christian scholarship, except within the confines of a few university divinity schools. Ought they, if they aspire to be truly pluralistic, at least attempt to include openly Christian scholars on their faculties in recognition of the many Christian sub-cultures among their constituents? What about at state schools? Or what of church-related colleges in which there is still a substantial relationship to the churches? Is there any compelling reason why they should be expected to turn away from concerns about faith and learning as a condition for recognition of academic excellence? At Catholic universities and colleges such questions are often sharply debated, as they are at many Protestant church-related colleges. So long as the very idea of Christian scholarship is questioned, the cultural forces encouraging abandonment of distinctive religious outlooks will almost certainly prevail. If, on the other hand, scholars of Christian and other faiths can embrace the vision of the positive contribution faith can make to learning, then perhaps we can enter a creative era of reassessing the assumptions that have shaped our culture's dominant higher education during the past century.

My hope is that the present volume will be a small contribution toward that new consciousness.

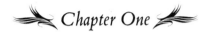

# Chapter One

## Why Christian Perspectives
## Are Not Welcomed

A few years ago a professor of religion at a major private university remarked to me that he believed it was inappropriate for anyone who practiced a particular religion to teach about that religion.[1] To do so, he thought, would be to transgress standards of scientific detachment required for the proper study of religion.

One can imagine the response to some parallel proposals. What if someone suggested that no feminist should teach the history of women, or no gay person teach gay studies, or no political liberal should teach American political history? Or—for those who see religion as mainly praxis—perhaps the analog should be that no musician should be allowed to teach an instrument that she herself plays.

It is rare, I believe, to carry to such an extreme the ideal of scholarly detachment from religious perspectives. Nonetheless, the plausibility of such an extreme view is possible only because weaker versions of the rule are so widespread. Many contemporary academics affirm as dogma that the only respectable place for religion in the academy is as an object of study. Suggestions that religious perspectives might be relevant to interpretation in other fields are viewed with puzzlement or even consternation.

One of the historical questions I have asked is why that should be the case. Why do we have a dominant academic culture that typically teaches young scholars that to suggest that their faith might be relevant to their scholarship is a fatal breach of good taste? Why is self-censorship concerning explicit religious identification so taken for granted?[2] Why do even many Christian scholars accept such academic standards as a matter of course? One scholar at a Christian institution said it took ten years of teaching to unlearn the lessons from his graduate training that he should suppress his faith. Why do we have an educational system where such acculturation of believers does not seem remarkable?

### THE HISTORICAL ARGUMENT

I have written a good deal about the historical developments that brought us to this point,[3] and will present here just a capsule version of the main themes. The central theme is that the current suspicions of Christian perspectives in the academy are reactions—often understandable—to the long establishment of Christianity in higher education. America's pace-setting universities were products of liberal Protestant culture. By "liberal Protestant" I mean a culture that took for granted Protestantism as one significant part of its heritage, but was "liberal" in that it emphasized the unifying moral dimensions of its spiritual heritage, rather than the particulars of traditional Protestant doctrine. Today's pace-setting American universities were virtually all constructed in the late nineteenth and early twentieth century by liberal Protestants.

Most of the first generation of university builders were New Englanders who had grown up during the Civil War era and were inspired by ideals that paralleled those of the Yankee cause in the Civil War. They were interested in building a great unified civilization that was founded both on the highest moral ideals to which all should conform and on the latest techniques of advancing capitalist civilization. This combination of nationalist idealism and zeal for technological advance also characterized the Republican party to which almost all university leaders belonged.

The watchword of "freedom" was the touchstone of the civilization for which they were working. They saw themselves as standing for individual freedom and for freedom of inquiry. Freedom in their view was opposed to authoritarianism. In their view, freedom was an outgrowth of the best in the Protestant tradition as opposed to Catholic authoritarianism. So American universities were defined as havens for free scientific inquiry. The science which would be the model for most of the disciplines would have to be free from appeals to supernaturally based authority. In effect, science would have to be defined purely naturalistically. This sharp limit on the bounds of authoritative academic inquiry was not viewed by the university founders as in opposition to Christianity. Rather, they believed that scientific investigation would advance civilization and hence promote the kingdom of God. Naturalistic inquiry, furthermore, could be supplemented by humanistic moral ideals that also emphasized freedom and would advance Christian and democratic civilization.

Basic to this project of university building was a larger impulse for building a unified national culture based on high ideals, the same impulse that had led to the establishment of common schools. Groups such as Catholics, recalcitrant ethnic Protestants, and some Jews who felt that having their own schools was crucial to maintaining distinct identity were penalized for not participating in this national culture. They would have to pay for their own schools in addition to taxes for public education and would be looked down upon as vaguely disloyal.

The dominant Protestantism that set the national educational standards proclaimed its ideals to be "nonsectarian." That was necessary for building a unified culture. Such nonsectarianism discriminated not only against Catholics, but also, especially in the universities, against more traditionalist Protestantism. Protestantism that made a distinction between the saved and the lost, for instance, or that emphasized the exclusive authority of biblical revelation, was becoming an embarrassment to the unifying cultural project. The authority of naturalistic science, social science, and history validated the disparagement of traditional Protestantism and endorsed the superiority of nonsectarian liberal Protestant views.

The builders of the new universities were thus rejecting important dimensions of the older establishment in higher education. Until the nineteenth century, Western universities and colleges had almost always operated within theological boundaries. Theology had not usually been well integrated with the rest of the curriculum, but higher education at least took for granted a theistic point of reference. It also presumed a context of formal Christian worship, typically expressed through regular chapel services that began and ended the academic day.

The taken-for-granted aspect of the Christian context had the paradoxical effect of inhibiting the development of explicit Christian perspectives. Because a broadly Christian outlook could be presumed, not much effort was made to relate Christianity specifically to what was being studied. The pagan classics made up much of the curriculum, as they had since the Middle Ages. The modern subjects that had been added since the Enlightenment were viewed as areas for objective inquiry, with little reflection on Christianity's role in shaping the underlying assumptions. There were no well-developed schools of Christian academic thought outside of the field of theology itself. The Christian heritage was thus relatively easy to undermine academically. It had all the weaknesses of an establishment. It had built few intellectual defenses, since its monopoly had never been seriously challenged. When the generation that touted Darwin demonstrated that one could dispense with Christian assumptions (such as that the universe was designed by a personality) and still do first-rate academic work, few Christian apologists were prepared to debate the issue except on narrow theological grounds.[4]

In the United States before the Civil War the Christian educational establishment had the further disadvantage of being wed to a collegiate system that was unimpressive in everything but numbers of institutions. There were more than a hundred colleges in the United States, but none with more than a few hundred students. Most of the colleges had denominational connections, had clergymen as presidents and among their other faculty, and taught classical languages and literature and a smattering of modern subjects. Much about them needed to be reformed, and it was easy for the builders of the new universities in the later nineteenth century to jettison the particulars of their traditions of theology, worship, and regard for biblical authority along with their antiquated educational methods.

While those who set the academic standards for the new universities and modernized colleges were rejecting one establishment, they were building another. White male Protestants would continue to rule higher education, but now according to more inclusive national standards. Their moral idealism, affirmations of the Western cultural heritage,[5] nationalism, faith in American republican and democratic ideals, and confidence in the universality of scientific judgments all contributed to their authority as arbiters of a national culture.

Admirable as most of these ideals may appear, we can also view them as part of a cultural imperialism. The late nineteenth and early twentieth century was the heyday of British and American imperialism. The building of a national university culture was part of the same impulse. Even if the imperialism was sometimes benign (as was the moral imperialism that had abolished slavery in the American South), its effects were the same. Local and parochial cultures would have to give way to more advanced and more universal moral and scientific ideals.

At the beginning of the twentieth century, the unified cultural ideal was regarded as broadly Christian. While the sciences had won their autonomy from the framework of Christian assumptions, and the social sciences were likewise coming to be defined in purely naturalistic terms, the leaders of higher education still thought of themselves as working within a Christian context. The turn of the century was a time when philosophical and political idealism were at their height. While scientific and technological values might seem to undermine higher meaning, they were complemented by faith in transcendent moral ideals that could be realized in the progress of national civilization. Woodrow Wilson, president of Princeton University in the first decade of the century, provides a good example. While he curtailed explicitly Christian teaching at Princeton in favor of more professionalized scholarship, he still preached the higher moral ideals that would make young men fit to serve democracy and hence Christian civilization.

During the first half of the twentieth century talk about the "Christian" character of the academic enterprise diminished, as it was increasingly recognized that to identify the project with any one religious tradition would be divisive. Religion came to be regarded as essentially an extra-curricular activity. Mainline Protestants built up ministries on the edges of campus and welcomed Catholics and Jews to do the same. Such explicit religious reference as there may have been in the classrooms became correspondingly more rare as student bodies became more diverse and more disciplines tried to define themselves as "scientific."

While higher education was still supposed to teach higher ideals, by the 1940s and 1950s these were usually spoken of as "Judeo-Christian," or "the Western cultural heritage," or simply "Western democratic ideals of the 'free world.'" Through the 1950s such ideals were seen as the basis for building a national consensus of shared values that were essentially secular, but were still also regarded as in harmony with the common theistic and moral teachings in the heritages of Protestants, Catholics, and Jews. World War II and the menaces of Nazism and Soviet Communism had added urgency to the search for a common spiritual base for Western civilization. Liberal Protestants still dominated the cultural mainstream, but they encouraged persons of other religious faiths to join them in affirming those aspects of their heritages that harmonized well with the ideals of a democratic consensus undergirded by the supposedly unifying authority of scientific methodology.

During the 1960s this "establishment" came under attack, an attack that focused on the dominance of white male Anglo-Protestants. It stressed the sociological features of this dominance, since the religious dimensions were no longer prominent. It criticized the idea of a moral consensus when in fact one ethno-religious and gender group had dominated that consensus. On the intellectual front the idea of objectivity came under attack. The ideal of scientific objectivity had been, of course, a crucial component of an effort to establish a unified culture. Science, it had been thought, would unify people as they were educated to give up their local and parochial prejudices.

Despite the attacks on objectivity and on the old "establishment," the dominant academic culture that emerged from the cultural upheaval of the 1960s retained much of the impulse to unify that had characterized its predecessors of the 1950s. The leadership would now be more diversified as white males would be forced to share their power, but the essential structures and impulses shaping academia preserved continuity with the past. In fact the period after 1960 saw a vast expansion both of mass education and of the government's role in education. Both these forces increased the institutional pressures toward standardization and conformity.

The university culture that emerged by the 1980s differed from that of the 1950s in a number of ways that are significant to our inquiry. First, other than in the divinity schools of some private universities, there was less room than ever for explicit religious perspectives in the classrooms.[6] Despite the attacks on scientific objectivity, and despite increased tolerance for some ideological perspectives, the prejudices against traditional religious perspectives as violating canons of academic respectability were stronger than ever. Old secular liberals and postmoderns, despite their differences, typically agreed that acceptable theories about humans or reality must begin with the premise that the universe is a self-contained entity. As always there were significant exceptions, but for many academics the idea of Christian perspectives seemed hopelessly old-fashioned or even bizarre.

Another relevant change since the 1950s has been an increased emphasis on diversity. This laudable ideal is an extension of the liberal impulse of the 1950s to push for racial integration. During the 1960s some minority groups questioned the assimilationist implications of "integration," and soon "multiculturalism" and "diversity" became the standard terms. As many have observed, however, "diversity" as it is used today is a highly ambiguous term.[7] Minority cultures today typically are internally divided between impulses to define a separate identity and aspirations to participate fully as equals in a national culture in which they help set standards by which everyone should abide. As anyone who looks at current efforts to promote multiculturalism can see, the tensions between "integration" and "diversity" have not been resolved. The ambiguity becomes apparent when we realize how many institutional policies of recent decades have foundered in the oxymoronic quest for uniform national standards of diversity.

One crucial theme of this brief historical review, then, is that, despite some important changes since the 1950s, American university culture is still shaped by a powerful impulse toward homogeneity and uniformity. Like the universities of the original liberal Protestants of the late nineteenth century, there is an almost irresistible zeal to integrate all Americans into a dominant cultural ideal. American higher education has been aptly compared to a snake-like procession. It is difficult to tell where it is headed, yet we can be sure that all the parts will follow the head wherever it leads. Despite the diversity of its origins, our higher education is increasingly under pressure toward standardization and uniformity.[8]

The strength of this impulse grows out of the necessity to assimilate so many diverse peoples. One of the great American accomplishments is that we have in most cases been able to keep the peace while absorbing diverse cultures. We have avoided the kind of fragmentation among ethno-religious cultures that we see in the former Marxist lands. We have not been plagued by religious warfare the way so many parts of the world have. Moreover, in an advanced capitalist culture there are many financial and institutional advantages to uniformity. In particular, there are advantages in keeping volatile and irreconcilable religious claims from disrupting public life.

These accomplishments help foster peace and relative prosperity. Like all human achievements, however, they have their downside. In university culture one important byproduct is strong pressures against any substantial intellectual role for explicit religious perspectives. Such biases have been part of the picture ever since the rise of American universities and have continued to grow, at least until very recently. This discrimination is often subtle and complex. Much of it might more properly be described as marginalization, some of which did not grow out of any overt prejudice against religion. Early in this century it became the norm that mainstream religious practices (mainline Protestant, Catholic, and Jewish) would be encouraged as extra-curricular activities while Christian expressions were dropped from the classrooms. This arrangement has often been regarded as friendly to religion. Indeed, the resulting opportunities for voluntary worship, religious community, and service through campus ministries are immensely valuable and ought to be preserved. So far as *academic* life itself is concerned, however, these activities are quite literally marginalizing. They are expected to be kept in their own places and not to have an appreciable impact on intellectual life.

In his widely read *The Culture of Disbelief,* Yale law professor Stephen Carter offers some helpful observations on this point. Writing about American culture in general, Carter observes that the problem is not so much discrimination against religion in public life, but its trivialization. Americans express their religious sentiments in public about as freely as in any modern society ("I just want to thank the Lord that my curve ball was breaking real good tonight.") But the religious rhetoric seldom amounts to anything. Religious belief, says Carter, is most often treated as though it were a harmless hobby, like building model airplanes or sailboarding. Although even politicians may be expected to invoke God in their rhetorical flourishes, religion is expected to be an essentially private affair. Not only that, says Carter, but its values and practices are often expected to be subordinate to the higher values promoted by the state. Religious groups are increasingly regarded by the law as existing at the sufferance of the government. If religious scruples conflict with state regulations, increasingly the presumption is that mere religious principles should give way to more universally held standards.[9]

In academic life, the forces determining the status of religion are a little more complex. "Trivialization" is nonetheless a helpful way to describe how religion is usually treated in academic life. While it is recognized as a legitimate extra-curricular activity, so far as the academic dimensions of a university are concerned, it is expected to have no more importance than would membership in a bridge club. Bridge players are not discriminated against in the university; it's just that their pastime is irrelevant to academic life.

The negative treatment of religion in mainstream academic life is more substantially based, however, than the term "trivialization" suggests. Some of the rules of the academic game were shaped directly by the desire to exclude most religious perspectives. The reason was that Christianity had long been used as an instrument of rule in higher education; in order to reform education in the late nineteenth century Christianity had to be disarmed. Alasdair MacIntyre in his *Three Rival Versions of Moral Inquiry* provides an insightful analysis of these dynamics in Great Britain. The universities of England and Scotland had been controlled by the state churches, and the great academic battles of the 1860s and 1870s were to free the universities from religious tests. At the same time progressive academics were attempting to establish definitive encyclopedic accounts of the progress of knowledge to date, as presented for instance in the Ninth Edition of the *Encyclopaedia Britannica*. This knowledge would be based on the uniform application of scientific method to all areas of inquiry. Thus, says MacIntyre, "the Encyclopaedia would have displaced the Bible as the canonical book, or set of books, of the culture."[10] As in America during the same era, in Britain too science was opposed to "sect." Scientific knowledge was universal and nonsectarian. Religiously based belief was parochial, sectarian, and divisive.

While a line was thus drawn between religion and any academic inquiry that purported to be scientific, the issue was not at first framed so bluntly as a choice between science and religion. Rather, it was usually represented as an arrangement by which one could have *both* science and religion—each, however, within its proper domain. In the United States during the first two-thirds of the twentieth century liberal religious views that fit nicely into this scheme were found here and there within mainstream academia. Such beliefs, usually liberal Christian, were viewed not as divisive but rather as combining the best cultural and ethical ideals with a sense that there was a transcendent realm that science could not grasp.[11] Even today such broadly religious viewpoints are not excluded from mainstream academia, but their presence is much less conspicuous and it has become rare to identify them as explicitly Christian.

The rise of religion departments in many universities during the mid-twentieth century originally had as part of its rationale the promotion of such broadly Christian or Judeo-Christian ideals. Religion could be viewed as a special field for scientific study, but also as a source of inspiration going beyond science. Usually the religion taught was broadly ecumenical and interfaith, allowing little room for more traditional versions of Protestantism, Catholicism, or Orthodox Judaism.

During the 1960s and the 1970s the field of religion continued to grow, but in order to establish its academic credibility, it was increasingly marked by an emphasis on the scientific study of religion and decreasingly seen as a haven in the universities, or even in mainstream church-related colleges, for religious perspectives. The leaders in the field of religious studies now more often presented it as analogous to the social sciences rather than to the uplifting humanities, such as literature.[12] The transformation in religious studies since the early 1960s had some parallels in the field of literature. Literature was no longer regarded first of all as uplifting, as it had been in the 1950s, but rather became a field whose academic status was legitimated by technical methodologies, often evidenced by esoteric terminology. Segments of religious studies followed similar paths, transforming themselves into cultural study and the comparative studies of the history of religions.

The new religious studies raised the academic credibility of the field and brought fresh insights on many religious phenomena. From the point of view of our own inquiry, however, they must be seen as part of the wider trend of insistence that the only place for religion in the mainstream academy is as an object of study. That trend has led to some confusion in the discussion of religious perspectives in the classroom because some people assume that the issue is about having more religion courses. That popular misconception was encapsulated in the headline for one journal's discussion of the topic: "Are American Colleges Biased Against Religion . . . Or Are They Receptive to the Study of Religion?"[13]

The idea of Christian scholarship does not have to do primarily with religious studies, although that is one field where the presence or absence of Christian perspectives will be most immediately evident. Rather, Christian perspectives can have influence on any academic discipline when it comes to questions of larger meaning. The historical reasons why mainstream college and university culture have not had much place for self-consciously Christian perspectives in fields like politics, history, sociology, psychology, economics, literature, and so forth have to do with fact that a broadly Christian ethos (the assumption, for instance, that there was a Creator who authorized moral law) was largely taken for granted through about the end of nineteenth century. Then, in the twentieth century an essentially secular ethos (no assumption, for instance, of a Creator or transcendent authorization of moral tradition) came to be just as typically taken for granted. In neither setting was there much encouragement for mainstream academics to reflect on what difference Christian outlooks would make in their various fields.

This history of the role of religion in American universities, like so much of human experience, has an ironic twist. On the one hand, the displacement of traditional Christianity from the privileged position it held in nineteenth-century academia is readily understandable. Christianity had long been part of a cultural establishment that controlled higher education. Until the late nineteenth century traditional Christianity was often used to limit academic inquiry. At more conservatively religious schools traditional Christianity was often part of a defensive posture and was sometimes taught in heavy-handed ways. Academic reformers fought against these restrictive religious establishments and eventually dismantled those that had the greatest cultural influence. This was part of the larger process of the disestablishment of Protestantism as the semi-official religion in America. Insofar as it was a disestablishment this process seems not only understandable, but also laudable, even from most of today's Christian perspectives. In order for this disestablishment to be complete, as twentieth-century liberal Protestant leaders gradually realized, it was not enough simply to broaden Protestantism while keeping it in a privileged position. In institutions that claimed to serve the whole society, *no* explicitly religious viewpoint could be privileged without discriminating against the views of other religions.

This passion for disestablishment, nondiscrimination, and justice, however, eventually led to an ironic result. Explicitly Christian views had been the problem, so eliminating them had seemed the solution. An understandable reaction had become an over-reaction. Furthermore, the tendency to view religious perspectives as being in bad taste, which had developed in much of academic culture during the gradual disestablishment, persisted even after the disestablishment was complete. Today there is no realistic prospect for the reestablishment of the dominance of Christianity in America's leading universities. Yet the biases against speaking about Christian perspectives persist. In effect, in place of a Protestant establishment we now have a virtual establishment of nonbelief. University culture is not necessarily hostile to religion; but the norm for people to be fully accepted in academic culture is to act as though their religious beliefs had nothing to do with education. Scholars are expected to analyze subjects such as the nature of reality, beauty, truth, morality, the just society, the individual, and the community as though deeply held religious beliefs had no relevance to such topics. Scholars who themselves have no traditional religious beliefs are given every advantage, since their lack of belief corresponds with the stance that every right-thinking educated person is expected to adopt. Theories that are based on the supposition that there is no God are therefore much more likely to flourish in academia than are theories based on the contrary supposition.

It is easy to see why academia came to be constructed in a way in which religious perspectives typically seem out of place. Life may be more peaceful without the discussion of such issues. And if all religions are discriminated against, it assures that none is being given special privilege. In fact, however, nonreligious viewpoints are thereby given special privilege.

Religious-political conservatives who complain about the establishment of "secular humanism" are partially correct. Before militant conservatives made the concept sensational, the term had been regarded as a perfectly legitimate label for certain academic trends.[14] The militants, however, have hurt their case, both by overstating it and by acting as if the present situation were the result of the conscious design of anti-religious conspirators. It is true that many secular academics have had a strong interest in eliminating overt religious considerations in academia; but the principal forces bringing about this result have not come from a conspiracy of secularists. Rather they have come from both Christians and non-Christians who have reacted—and now overreacted—to the problems of having a quasi-established religion in a pluralistic modern society.

These understandable origins, however, do not justify the result. Our society has corrected an old problem and in so doing created a new one. Today nonreligious viewpoints hold the advantage in academia so that something very much like "secular humanism" is informally established as much as Christianity was in the nineteenth century. The religious right does not help by suggesting, in effect, that we go back to a Christian establishment. That is not the only alternative and it is not a desirable one. Rather, we should recognize that we are dealing with an over-correction and look for a way to restore a better balance among both religious and nonreligious voices.

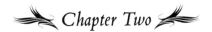

# Chapter Two

# The Arguments for Silence

## SCIENCE VS. RELIGION

Not long ago the Ohio State University alumni magazine devoted an article to the question of whether a professor might openly identify his or her religious perspectives as a relevant part of teaching. Such an article, like the fact that at least one Ohio State professor of sociology has been telling his students of his Christian faith (in part as acknowledging a bias they should take into account), may be a significant straw in the wind suggesting that times are changing. Nonetheless, reports of even such restrained efforts to introduce Christian perspectives inevitably bring indignant reactions. Aside from outcries about "church and state" (which we shall consider shortly), the most predictable reactions will be sweeping dismissals of religious perspectives as insufficiently empirical. So one Ohio State professor of philosophy was reported as saying that

> any personal beliefs—religious or otherwise—that are discussed in the classroom have to be supported by evidence, and that evidence should meet the standards of the profession. But faith is, by definition, a belief in that for which there is no proof: once a belief can be supported by independent, scientific evidence, it loses its religious nature. . . . when considering any theory, "the evidence has to carry the day, not the fact that it is Christian."[1]

It is as though, so far as religion is concerned, we are still at the high noon of the Enlightenment faith in science. This is somewhat puzzling in the light of other intellectual trends, long present in Western thought but widespread since the 1960s, which have pilloried "the Enlightenment project" and claims to simple empirical standards for truth. Given the current prestige of such assaults on empirically based objective standards for all truth, one might think that it would be out of fashion to dismiss all religious perspectives on the ground that they cannot be decisively confirmed on empirical grounds. Even among academic moderates who have little patience with postmodern fads, the idea of scientific objectivity as an obtainable standard for the larger questions of life is generally considered passé.[2] Yet when the subject of religion is mentioned, the categories of Enlightenment skepticism seem to be miraculously resuscitated.

Perhaps the invocations of the authority of science against religion persist because they were so much part of an academic orthodoxy of a generation ago. While leading American thinkers of the first half of the twentieth century rejected eighteenth-century versions of faith in science, they retained the broad principle that reliance on scientific method was the key to progress. The era from the 1870s through the 1950s could be well described as the era of scientific positivism in American academic history. John Dewey was the quintessential American academic of that time. Starting out in the late nineteenth century with a faith in a Christian idealism that stood above empirical science, Dewey came to adopt the essential formula of Auguste Comte's earlier "positivism." Like Comte, Dewey regarded human history as an evolutionary advance from primitive eras when religion reigned to modern times when the triumph of scientific method marked highest stages of human achievement.[3]

Enlightenment dreams to replace religious authority with scientific authority persisted until the mid-twentieth century. Many rank-and-file scholars of this era, as a recent history of the American historical profession has shown, freely described their work as "objective."[4] While many of those scholars would also have allowed room for a higher, transcendent realm, only a few challenged the prevailing wisdom that in their professional scholarship objective methodology should exclude religious concerns. By the mid-twentieth century the dominant voices in the social sciences were especially insistent that religious perspectives had no place in their scholarship. In Anglo-American philosophy many scholars followed the lead of logical positivists such as A. J. Ayer, who in his widely read *Language, Truth, and Logic* (1936) wrote that, strictly speaking, God-talk was nonsense since it was based on neither logic nor empirical evidence.

Along the leading edges of American intellectual life since the 1960s, trends have gone strongly against the old faith in such universalized and objective scientific methodology. Especially since a new philosophy of science was popularized by Thomas Kuhn in *The Structure of Scientific Revolutions* (1962), many prominent scholars have agreed that science typically operates within frameworks of assumptions that are not themselves established on scientific grounds. In the humanities in recent years much of the most heralded scholarship has been directed toward attacking the assumption that there should be one objective, scientifically based outlook on which all fair-minded people should agree. It is now commonplace among contemporary scholars, including many moderate liberal scholars, to acknowledge that, while empirical investigation should be valued in its place, pretheoretical influences such as social location substantially shape interpretations in the humanities and social science. Almost everyone concedes, for example, that being an African American or Native American makes a difference in how some things are perceived. One might think, therefore, that it would be relatively easy to gain agreement that, since strongly held religious views are often part of one's social location, religious perspectives should be accepted as playing potentially legitimate roles in academic interpretation. Nonetheless, residual prejudices against religious viewpoints as inherently unscientific seem to persist as a dominant academic paradigm.

If we view the question historically, it is easy to see why the "science versus religion" stereotype is so deeply etched in the minds of many academics. Modern universities took shape in an era when many cultural leaders believed that science provided the most valuable standard for truth because it provided conclusions on which all fair-minded observers could agree. It was the ultimate in nonsectarianism. People of all faiths, if they would free their minds from elementary prejudices, would be compelled by scientific demonstration. This ideal was extended from the natural sciences to many other areas of scholarship. If only people would enter the academic arena with minds freed from prejudices they could work together on the basis of exclusively naturalistic assumptions that they all shared. Scholars of diverse backgrounds could cooperate by agreeing to regard reality as the product of natural forces suitable to empirical investigation by common standards. So the rule evolved that to be part of the mainstream academic profession one had to lay one's religious faith aside. Some scholars still hold on to this rule dogmatically, at least when the subject of religion is mentioned.

The rule fails, however, on at least four counts. The first is that attempts to extend the empirical model of natural science to other fields of academic inquiry have failed to unite people on the larger questions concerning society and human relationships. Contemporary academia is just as divided on these larger questions as it was in eras when ruled by contending religious faiths. On the larger questions of life, empirical science is not competent to provide definitive answers, so academia is ruled largely by secular sects motivated by political interests. The idea that reliance on empirical scientific models will eliminate sectarianism is simply false.

The second defect in the rule that academic beliefs must be empirically based is that it is not applied consistently to other nondemonstrable beliefs that play prominent roles in the secular academy. For instance, contemporary academics base many judgments on their deeply held beliefs in the value of equal treatment for people regardless of gender or race. Most of them believe that it would be wrong to kill infants. Most likely they would agree that it is good to teach students to be especially concerned for the poor and the handicapped. These beliefs are not derived from scientific argument. Rather, they are moral commitments that are prevalent in many contemporary communities. Scholars who are committed to such communities bring these moral perspectives with them into their academic work. Scholars may indeed use empirical arguments to bolster their beliefs in these values, but ultimately these beliefs are held as inviolable, sacred truths and are not up for reconsideration. Such moral beliefs shape their scholarship in important ways, often determining what they choose to study and how they evaluate human relationships.

So far as dependence on empirical verification is concerned, many religious beliefs fall in the same category. Religious people may see in the immensity of the universe evidence confirming their belief in a creator, but they cannot empirically prove that point. On the other hand, neither can one prove the opposite. Yet the equally undemonstrable supposition that there is no creator is routinely accepted in academic inquiry. So there seems to be no consistent academic rule that all beliefs must be empirically grounded and hence that all religiously derived beliefs can be excluded on the grounds that they are "non-empirical."

A third problem with the rule that religious perspectives should be excluded as non-empirical is that it cannot be done. Since lots of academics are religious, their religious beliefs will inevitably shape some of their scholarship. The actual rule is not that religious beliefs are excluded because they are irrelevant to scholarship—they are relevant to many issues—but that academics should *act* as though they are irrelevant. Because religious beliefs are alleged to belong to a special non-empirical category, scholars are urged to keep quiet about those beliefs and not reflect on the actual relationships of their beliefs to their scholarship.

That leads to the fourth and most significant defect of the rule—it unduly favors scholarship based on purely naturalistic presuppositions. It is worth repeating that this rule is not itself a conclusion of empirical investigation. Rather it is a working premise that has been widely successful in much of natural science and which is therefore proposed as a standard for all disciplines. Because this premise has a privileged position in so much of academia, it is common for scholars to draw conclusions from their investigations that are actually based on the premise, rather than on the investigations themselves. There are many classic examples. One is that Freudian psychologists have provided plausible psychological accounts of the origins of religious belief. From these some, including Freud himself, have gone on to proclaim a worldview from which the supernatural is excluded. A Christian or other religious scholar can concede, of course, that there are some observable psychological reasons why some people are more inclined to religious beliefs than others. Nevertheless, it does not follow that the naturalistic explanation is the whole explanation—unless that is your premise.

In such debates, however, modern academia has favored those who promote wholly naturalistic worldviews because such outlooks are more consistent with the working rules of much of the academy than are religious perspectives. This exclusively naturalistic outlook, furthermore, tends to favor one way of human knowing—the empirical—at the expense of all the rest.

This way of putting it oversimplifies the situation, however, because modern academia has typically complemented scientific modes of thinking with "higher" types of human expression, particularly in literature and the arts. There are ways of knowing, it has been affirmed in our high culture—ways involving creativity, personal, moral, and aesthetic sensibilities—that transcend the merely empirical.[5] These have gained an honored spot in the academic curriculum, particularly in the form of the literary canon. Such higher ideals were also usually built around exclusively naturalistic premises. The celebration of transcendent human achievement served as a substitute for traditional religion.

Exclusively naturalistic worldviews, then, have not necessarily favored exclusively scientific models for finding truth. An alternative version of pure naturalism, favored in literary criticism, much of modern philosophy, and in postmodern modes of thought is what Alvin Plantinga calls "creative anti-realism."[6] Rejecting the naive realism that holds that our minds copy what is "really out there," these schools of thought emphasize the creative activity of the human mind in imposing its categories, which are necessary to whatever we call "reality." Some historic versions of this outlook, growing out of the philosophy of Immanuel Kant, have been used to support religious views. Most contemporary versions, however, are based on naturalistic evolutionary worldviews that regard the human mind as essentially an adaptive mechanism which creates the "reality" it finds useful for survival. So even though modern academia may be divided between those who favor scientific models for knowing and those who endorse creative anti-realist models (and variations and combinations of these), most academics are united in taking a purely naturalistic worldview as their starting point. Not surprisingly, this naturalistic starting point leads them to purely naturalistic conclusions.

Christians and other believers who reject the dominant naturalistic biases in the academy would be foolish to do so in the name of postmodern relativism. What they should be arguing is that the contemporary academy *on its own terms* has no consistent grounds for rejecting all religious perspectives. If postmodernists who denounce scientific objectivism as an illusion are well accepted in the contemporary academy, there is little justification for the same academy to continue to suppress religious perspectives because they are "unscientific." Christians, however, need to challenge relativistic postmodern anti-realist naturalism just as much as the older objectivist naturalism. Both these parties start with purely naturalistic assumptions and make these normative for good scholarship. Christians need to challenge these assumptions and to suggest that scholarship might just as responsibly take place within the framework of the assumptions that God has created an ordered reality. Far from being relativistic, this is a claim that our experience makes best sense if we realize that we are in a universe of truths sustained by God, even if humans can glimpse these truths only imperfectly.

The intellectual groundwork for this alternative to scientific objectivism and postmodern relativism has already been well laid. Some of the leading figures in American philosophy have addressed these very issues. Organized in the Society of Christian Philosophers, they have changed the outlook of this fundamental discipline. In the mid-twentieth century, when logical positivism reigned in philosophy, religious statements were widely relegated to the realm of the unverifiable and hence unintelligible. Today many philosophers consider such preemptory dismissals of religious claims indefensible.[7] It is ironic, in the light of popular academic prejudices against religiously based thought, that it is in the field of philosophy, especially the philosophy of religion and epistemology, that Christian thinkers have made the greatest impact. Philosophers who have delved deeply into issues such as empirical warrant for one's beliefs have undercut the popular notion that religious beliefs should be excluded on the grounds that they necessarily fail to meet criteria of scientific verifiability. While the work of Christian philosophers shows what can be done through first-rate scholarship, their message has as yet failed to filter down to many scholars in other fields.[8]

## MULTICULTURALISM AND DIVERSITY

In a symposium held by the American Society of Church History on the topic of whether scholars should be more open about expressing religious perspectives, one panelist pointed to what is the heart of the issue for many scholars. He depicted the reaction of a gay colleague when told that conservative Christians were seeking a greater voice in the mainstream academy. The gay scholar felt extremely uncomfortable about this proposal, seeing in it the potential for reversal of some hard-won gains for diversity and tolerance. Conservative Christians, in his view, had long been the oppressors and the quieting of their voices could only be viewed as a gain.[9]

This is what may be called the multiculturalist reaction to the appeal for more openly Christian scholarship. Not only gays and lesbians, but also many feminist and Marxist scholars may react in this way. So do some ex-fundamentalists. Many Jewish scholars likewise are understandably wary of any suggestion of resurgent Christian influence. In the view of such scholars the issue is more a matter of politics and power than of abstract principle. Jewish scholars might readily support Jewish studies centers where scholars openly advocated Zionism and the preservation of Jewish practice. On the other hand, they might ardently defend separation of church and state in this country and oppose overt expressions of Christian perspectives. The difference in their minds is that Christians have been the oppressors and, as the majority in this country, are not to be trusted. One can easily understand how radical feminists, lesbians, gays, or even advocates of sheer secularism might feel the same way. These groups are represented by some of the most powerful lobbies in the academy and typically see traditional Christianity as one of the powers from which the world needs to be liberated.

Christianity was long the official religion in the Western world; even after it was disestablished in nineteenth-century America, Protestants were dominant in a more informal cultural establishment. In twentieth-century America, as we have seen, this informal establishment was largely dismantled in the interest of promoting diversity and equality in public life. This second disestablishment has involved an overreaction against religious viewpoints in public life so that we are now at a point where in the name of multiculturalism we have silenced some of our major sub-cultures.

Might not the fear of resurgent Christian imperialism be justified? At least we can understand the fears of gays, lesbians, radical feminists, Jews, ex-fundamentalists, secularists, Marxists, and others who oppose any recovery of power for traditional Christianity. We should take these concerns seriously. In fact, there are real differences on fundamental questions of morality between some of these groups and traditional Christians. Gays, lesbians, and radical feminists take stands on homosexuality and abortion that are incompatible with viewpoints of traditional Catholics and many other conservative Christians. Academic struggles over such issues take place in a cultural context of bitter contests over moral standards for public policy. So the issues cannot be resolved simply by tolerance and learning to get along better. The fact is that many contenders on the various sides of such debates are imperialistic in the sense of wanting to set the moral standards for all of society.

Granting that there is some basis for concern about resurgent Christian imperialism, we should ask whether such concerns are sufficient to justify the effective silencing of traditional Christian voices in much of mainstream academic culture. From the point of view of promoting a diverse society, the answer is clearly "no." That answer is clear because to answer "yes" would be to endorse the concerted imperialism of groups who wish to exclude traditional Christianity from public expression. Simple equity suggests that all sides deserve some protection. So far as public institutions such as mainstream universities are concerned, the problem is how to balance fairly the interests of the various sides in an era when basic cultural values are often sharply debated.

Fears of the resurgent Christian political right, however, fuel the prejudice that Christianity should be put in a special category of imperialism to be guarded against. Some Christian conservative political leaders indeed talk like imperialists rather than pluralists. If we are to believe their rhetoric, they do not only want to be one voice among many in the academic marketplace. They would like to have the power to repress some of the divergent voices that have gained a place in the public domain.

A number of points need to be made to counter such fears. The first is that the vast majority of religious conservatives do not speak in this imperialistic way and in fact are committed to playing by the basic rules of liberal polity when acting in the public domain (including most of higher education). Certainly Catholicism has reconciled itself to liberal polity in this century. Only a generation ago it was widely held that Catholicism was incompatible with liberal politics and separation of church and state. Those accusations were based on some of the official pronouncements from nineteenth-century Rome. They did not, however, fit the attitudes of most American Catholics, who readily embraced American political principles.

American fundamentalism is even more inextricably bound up with American liberal polity. Most fundamentalists are Baptists and so heirs to a heritage that includes separation of church and state dating back to Roger Williams. Almost all have adopted American principles of tolerance and civility. In fact the principal difference between American Protestant fundamentalism and most of the so-called "fundamentalisms" of other world religions is the degree to which the American movement is committed to modern liberal ideals as well as to militant Christianity. So, even though some of their political rhetoric is illiberal and intolerant, the movement has always been deeply ambivalent regarding liberal ideals.[10]

So conservative religious movements are like most other American movements that compete for voices within public domains. There are indeed some religious extremes that would be incompatible with the ground rules for a peacefully pluralistic culture, but most of conservative American Christianity is not of such an extreme sort. So while it is important to guard against religious extremists gaining power over the pluralistic public domain, the threat is not essentially different from that of secular or political extremists taking over. No entire set of outlooks should be excluded because of some extremes it includes.

A second consideration that should allay fears of the reestablishment of the exclusive dominion of Christian views in academia is that Christians are far too hopelessly divided for that to be possible. For every conservative religious voice that might gain a hearing in mainline academia there would be moderate and liberal religious voices to contradict it. Moreover, conservative Christian groups themselves are divided into a bewildering variety of sub-groups. Most African-American Christians, for instance, differ markedly from most conservative white Southern Baptists on many social issues, even though their theological beliefs may be similar. Mennonites oppose much of what the conservative Christian Coalition stands for. Even within conservative denominations there are differences on most issues. So there is no danger that Christian academics will be speaking with one voice or organizing to silence their opponents.

So far as the danger of imperialism is concerned, I think there is more danger of the imperialism of secularism excluding conservative Christian voices than of the reverse. It would be easy to overstate my point here; I do not want to imply that conservative Christian voices have been totally excluded from mainstream academia. They may be rare, but sometimes they indeed do get a hearing. That granted, it remains true that some powerful lobbies would like to see those voices silenced. Of course, the secular left should not be dismissed because of its extremes, but there is no doubt that some of the extremes wield substantial political power in academia.

The irony of the current situation is that much of the animus toward conservative religion comes in the name of multiculturalism and diversity.

There remains a deep ambiguity about the whole ideal of diversity in mainstream American culture. Is the goal "integration" or "diversity"? When it comes to religion in public life, the impulse for integration and uniformity typically overcomes diversity, despite the rhetoric to the contrary. Certainly this is the case in mainstream universities. Peoples of diverse cultures are welcomed into respectable academic culture, but only on the condition that they leave the religious dimensions of their cultures at the door. The result is not diversity, but rather a dreary uniformity. Everyone is expected to accept the standard doctrine that religion has no intellectual relevance.

African Americans, for example, are enthusiastically encouraged to enter the mainstream academy, but the condition typically has been that they do not bring the religious dimensions of their culture into intellectual life. Ever since African Americans began to be permitted to play a role in mainstream academic life, they were also sent the clear message that they must conform to the standards of the mainstream academy concerning religion. No matter how religious they might be, they were not encouraged to *think* about the implications of their religious beliefs for their intellectual life, unless they were studying in divinity schools.

The same has been true for every ethnic culture in America. Other than in their theological studies, ethnics soon learned that they were not to reflect publicly on the implications of their religious culture for understanding culture more broadly. Rather, they were encouraged to adopt a standardized stance of "neutrality" with respect to the implications of beliefs such as that God exists, that God created the world, that God might reveal himself to humans, or that God may have instituted a moral law. Such "neutrality," of course, is not neutrality at all, but rather conformity to the standards of a modern mainstream academic culture. In this area, at least, the claims to diversity and multiculturalism have masked the opposite.

Campus speech codes can exacerbate the problem. On the one hand, some codes explicitly mention religious views as among things to be tolerated. That may seem helpful, but the overall impact of the codes seems to be to create a culture of the offended, and religious speech is particularly vulnerable to causing offense. Hence, the overall effect can be simply to limit free speech.

The dangers of excessive zeal for tolerance were illustrated in the "Framework Regarding Prevention of Harassment and Discrimination in

Ontario Universities" that was to have gone into effect in 1994. This government policy would have banned any action that would create "an offensive, hostile, or intimidating climate for study or work." Offensive categories of speech included "race, ancestry, place of origin, colour, ethnic origin, citizenship, creed, sex, sexual orientation, disability, age, marital status, family status," and so forth. Furthermore, any party who felt offended on any of these grounds could bring a complaint that then would require judicial action. Well-meaning as these rules were, they would have had chilling implications for religious speech on campus. Fortunately, before they were put into effect, some religious academics and others pointed out their ominous character. As one commentator pointed out, if non-Christian students were offended by studying *Paradise Lost*, they presumably could have the book removed from a course syllabus. Or Muslim students could have a book by Salman Rushdie removed. Any indication of religious belief or bias on the part of a professor might result in judicial action initiated by students who felt such outlooks created a hostile environment. Implications of the rules for others areas of free speech were equally outrageous, and after a public outcry they were withdrawn.[11]

Free speech is, of course, not an absolute. All colleges and universities limit it on the basis of other values that they stand for. Even academic freedom, long hallowed in academic rhetoric, has always been limited by higher values such as "the common good."[12] Being sensitive to persons who differ from oneself is an essential component of academic civility, especially in dealing with students. However, impulses for multiculturalism, which grew out of the protests of the 1960s, have led to an academic culture of complaint. Policy on acceptable speech has been routinely determined by the groups who complain the loudest, rather than on the basis of considered reflection as to what would best promote justice. This has led to many absurd instances of repression of speech, as has been pointed out in debates over "political correctness."[13] The ironic result is that diverse expressions are not encouraged.

For our purposes the important point is that religious expressions are especially susceptible to restrictions in the name of multiculturalism. This is particularly true in classrooms, where religious expression has widely been discouraged for most of this century. Students might take offense at even the mildest expression of a teacher's religious perspective, even in the form of identification of one's biases. Unless a special effort is made to create an awareness that certain types of identification of religious perspective ought to be just as legitimate as expression of many other perspectives, such religious expression—which has not been protected well for generations—could succumb to the multiculturalist culture of complaint. The result would be one less element of diversity in mainstream academic life.

## CHURCH AND STATE

While religious expression tends to be vulnerable to recent multiculturalist complaints, it has also suffered from the old liberalism that dominated most of twentieth-century intellectual life. One of the strongest expressions of this prejudice has been the rise of the dogma of "separation of church and state." While during the first century and a half of the nation's history the anti-establishment clause of the First Amendment was interpreted in the narrow sense of prohibiting establishment of a national church, by the middle decades of the twentieth century strong political sentiment developed to use it to limit the role of religion generally in public life. Only in the past half-century or so has the phrase "the wall of separation of church and state" been elevated from a remark in Thomas Jefferson's correspondence to virtual constitutional status. Some Supreme Court Justices invoked it as the basis for their decisions and the phrase became a slogan for those who wished to insulate public life from direct religious influence. When this dogma gained ascendancy at mid-century its promoters were animated largely by anti-Catholic feeling, especially by resolve to keep government funds from going to support Catholic parochial schools. Added to that were concerns developing during the 1950s to eliminate most of the vestiges of the old Protestant religious privileges, such as required Bible reading and prayers in public schools.

During the next decades the courts established a set of guidelines that became known as "the Lemon test," from the supreme court case of *Lemon v. Kurtzman* in 1971. Any government aid to religion must have a secular purpose, must not advance religion, and must not excessively entangle the government in religion.[14] Such rulings have helped establish the widespread impression that in state-funded education (which is most education) any expression of religiously informed viewpoints is out of place.

In fact, popular opinion about the educational implications of "separation of church and state" often goes well beyond the law itself. Any rigorous application of the maxim of the "wall of separation" would lead to the exclusion of the religiously shaped views of far too many people. Courts have confirmed that teachers in public universities do have a right to refer to their own religious beliefs if those are relevant to the subject. Nonetheless, the legacy of the mid-twentieth-century liberalism, with its intimations that any religious expression may be challenged as a breach of the "wall" of separation of church and state, has helped perpetuate an atmosphere that inhibits religious expression in academic settings.[15]

Adding to the resolve both of old liberals and new multiculturalists to retain such strictly separationist interpretations of the law has been the rise of the Christian political right since the 1970s. The attempts of irrepressibly aggressive religious groups to insert their views into public education, regardless of their academic merits, have complicated the issues and made it more difficult for other religious groups to gain a hearing. To a large extent, it seems, the Christian right has coopted the use of "Christian" as an adjective. So when many people hear the word "Christian," what they think is "fundamentalist." That makes it very difficult for those of us who want to promote more moderate versions of Christian scholarship.

Regarding the delicate issue of the relationship between religion and government, the efforts of the Christian right often have a negative impact by promoting some solutions that seem to threaten principles of equity in the treatment of religion in public life. While the idea of a "wall" of separation carries the restriction of public religious expression to undue length, the ending of Protestant privilege made sense as a matter of equity. Fundamentalist efforts to establish privilege for their own narrow views would create a situation more unfair than in the days when bland generic Protestant viewpoints were the standard for public life.

I can illustrate with a case in which I was involved directly. In 1981 I was asked to testify as an "expert witness" against the Arkansas creation-science law. At first, when I heard that the American Civil Liberties Union was opposing the law, I thought that I would not want to be involved on the "secular" side of the dispute. Then I read the law. The law mandated that in Arkansas public schools, whenever the subject of origins was taught, evolutionary science had to be balanced with "creation science." On the face of it that sounded innocent enough. Who could be against balance? Should not Christians, who make up the majority of the population in Arkansas, have at least equal time on a subject so important as biological evolution, which is often used to undermine traditional biblical faith?

From a specifically Christian perspective, however, the law was misconceived in several respects. First, it was based on a false dichotomy between creation and evolution. It failed to take into account that Christians affirm not only that God created everything, but that God providentially controls how things develop. Creation and evolution are not mutually exclusive concepts, because God might have used some evolutionary means to shape his creation. Furthermore the Arkansas law went so far as to specify that the mandated teaching of "creation science" would involve the conclusion that the earth was only some thousands of years old and that the major geological strata were formed by a worldwide flood. Only some very conservative groups of Christians hold such views, and one wonders why their beliefs should be privileged by law, while those of all other religious groups are left out. In fact, many church groups joined in the protests against the law.

To make matters more confusing, despite the transparent origin of this sort of "creation science" in a literal reading of the Bible, the law dictated that these views should be presented simply as science, with no reference to God or biblical teaching. The "creation science" that would be taught largely consists of arguments that point to weaknesses in evolutionary theory. This approach is premised, in turn, on the original false dichotomy that there are only two positions, the recent immediate creation by God, or atheistic evolution. If atheistic evolution can be shown to be unsubstantiated, creation scientists suggest, then the biblical account is thereby demonstrated on purely scientific grounds to be the best one.[16]

As a Christian who affirms the authority of biblical teaching, I took a lot of criticism from fundamentalist and some conservative evangelical writers for my role in opposing this attempt to counter the teaching of naturalistic evolutionary doctrines in the schools. One prominent writer, in a chapter entitled "How to Become a Jellyfish," remarked that my testimony in Arkansas was "perhaps the most blatant case of evangelical sell-out." "With friends like these," he concluded, "who needs enemies?"[17]

Actually, my commitment to Christian scholarship was my main reason for opposing this law. Legitimate efforts to relate Christianity to academic life are hurt by such heavy-handed attempts to privilege by law a viewpoint of dubious intellectual merit that only a minority of Christians affirm. In my view there is no Christian teaching of more consequence for scholarship than that "God created the heavens and the earth." It is this doctrine that sets Christian perspectives against the purely naturalistic viewpoints which dominate mainstream academia. Biological evolution, moreover, has become a symbol for such pure naturalism, and is often used to ridicule believers who are so naive as to think that ultimately there may be design and purpose in the universe. Viewpoints that take into account the possibility of the divine origins of reality ought to be given a fair hearing in academia. People who believe that contemporary evolutionary theory has been overrated in the interest of supporting secular worldviews should be heard from as well. That is far less likely to happen, however, if the fundamentalists and their allies succeed in conveying the impression that the only alternative to the exclusion of God from the picture is a "creation science" based on a literalistic reading of Genesis. "Creation scientists" have done a great disservice to other Christian communities by coopting the term "creationism" for their own narrow views. They have compounded the disservice by attempting to use the state to mandate their sectarian teachings.

So we can grant that there is some basis for the concern that religious perspectives in academia might involve violation of proper boundaries between religion and the state. The First Amendment to the United States Constitution says that the government "shall make no law respecting an establishment of religion." While the framers would not have construed it so broadly, today it seems reasonable to say that mandating particular religious teachings in public education would constitute an establishment of religion in the sense of using state funds to privilege one religious viewpoint over others.

That is a long way, however, from endorsing the oft-cited formula of a "wall of separation" between church and state, which is nowhere contemplated in the Constitution and is a metaphor that has taken on a life of its own. Proponents of a strong definition of the separation of church and state say that any religious expression that is not justified by a predominantly "secular" purpose should be excluded from state-funded education. While some formulations of this rule would recognize that religious perspectives have a secular justification on the grounds that all responsible viewpoints should be heard, more stringent versions would eliminate all overt religious expression. The most critical problem with such proposals is that they run directly into two other provisions of the First Amendment, one guaranteeing the right to free speech and the other stating that the government shall not "prohibit the free exercise" of religion. As the Supreme Court seems to be beginning to recognize, any reasonable reading of the Bill of Rights should balance the modern application of these various provisions.[18]

It is time to rethink the usefulness of the phrase "church and state" in thinking about these issues. That way of putting it may be largely anachronistic. Today we have few churches with sufficient political power to be able to privilege their peculiar teachings by law. In some local regions there are vestiges of the political power of the Catholic Church, and Mormons wield political power in Utah and some neighboring states. Elsewhere the institutional "church" is not usually the relevant entity involved. At least it is not usually the most useful category with respect to our present topic of the permissibility of explicit religious perspectives in public education. Most often what we are talking about is individual scholars who wish to relate their religious beliefs to their scholarship. Their beliefs will likely be shaped by churches or other religious communities, but they do not typically represent the "church" in any legal sense. The religiously shaped scholarship of these individuals is better viewed as an expression of their own constitutionally guaranteed rights as citizens to free speech and to the free exercise of religion.

This distinction is important because too often in the popular view and among journalists the idea of "separation of church and state" is read as the "separation of all religion from the state." Having elevated the "wall" metaphor to constitutional status, these interpreters conclude that one of the duties of the state is to prohibit the free exercise of religious expression by citizens in any activity that is funded, in whole or in part, by the state.

Despite such popular assumptions, there is no legal reason why responsible expressions of religious perspectives should be systematically excluded from state-funded education. As with free speech, citizens do not lose their constitutional guarantee to free exercise of religion simply because they engaged in an activity funded by the government. As is true of free speech, however, certain restrictions on those freedoms are necessary or appropriate in certain jobs. In higher education, those restrictions ought to be determined by standards appropriate to that activity. So while formal worship might be permitted for voluntary groups meeting in campus buildings, it would not be appropriate as part of a class in a pluralistic university. Preaching and overt religious proselytizing would be inappropriate exercises of professorial power in a setting defined by the state's commitment to pluralism. As we shall discuss in the next chapter, teaching from religious perspectives would have to follow the academic rules appropriate to teaching from other perspectives. If, however, teachers' religious viewpoints are relevant to their academic interpretation, there is no reason why they should not have the freedom to say so.

Some teachers in state schools have recognized that this freedom exists, although explicit religious expressions are far more the exception than the rule. My own experience parallels that of the Ohio State sociologist, mentioned at the opening of this chapter, who identified his biases to his class. On two occasions I have had the privilege of teaching as a visiting professor at the University of California at Berkeley. The first time I taught there I had spent almost my entire teaching career at Calvin College, where there is a long tradition of Christian reflection on academic disciplines. How would I teach American religious history differently at Berkeley? What I decided was that early in the semester I would acknowledge my religiously informed viewpoint, presenting this disclosure as analogous to truth in advertising. Since everyone who teaches about religion has an interpretive bias, I said, students do not really benefit from teachers' posing as neutral objective observers, when in fact their interpretations reflect a particular point of view. So I told the students that they should be aware of my point of view. At times, I would be making interpretive statements, sometimes explicitly identified as reflecting my perspective. I would not expect anyone to agree with my more biased interpretations, and I would respect differing points of view. That approach seemed to work eminently well. No one, so far as I know, objected and many students told me they appreciated my frankness.

Strong prejudices against explicit introduction of religious perspectives into mainstream academic life arise from several directions simultaneously. Any proposal such as I am making in this book may draw indignant reaction on one of the following grounds: that it is unscientific, that it will offend someone in a pluralistic setting, or that it violates "separation of church and state." Each of these objections presents a formidable obstacle and in combination they represent prejudices that are difficult to surmount. Nevertheless, on examination, they prove to be just that—prejudices. None of them carries the compelling weight that would justify the widespread assumption that explicit religious perspective is inappropriate.

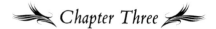

## Chapter Three

# Christian Scholarship and the Rules
# of the Academic Game

Stanley Fish, the *enfant terrible* of postmodernism, provides one of the most provocative critiques of the proposal for liberal inclusiveness to be extended to Christian perspectives. Commenting on works of Stephen Carter and Michael McConnell, as well as *The Soul of the American University,* Fish insists that our brands of Christianity are far too tame. Though secular himself, Fish cites the authority of John Milton to argue that true faith in God changes everything else. Reason, says Milton, following Augustine, is subject to prior faith. The world will look very different to those who start with faith in God in contrast to faith in self or in material contingency. It follows, Fish argues, that Christians, if they are serious about their faith, should not compromise with liberalism, which is built on antithetical principles:

> To put the matter baldly, a person of religious conviction should not want to enter the marketplace of ideas, but to shut it down, at least insofar as it presumes to determine matters that he believes have been determined by God and faith. The religious person should not seek an accommodation with liberalism; he should seek to rout it from the field, to extirpate it, root and branch.[1]

More moderate critics have expressed a milder version of the same concern. They worry that if we open up the mainstream academy to religious concerns we may be inviting the very sorts of attitudes that Fish advocates.

Such critics are uneasy about the subjectivism, fragmentation, and contentiousness that may undermine some of the hard-won achievements of the liberal academy. Granting that so-called Enlightenment models of scientific detachment do not provide the degree of objectivity once imagined, they are concerned as to what will happen if we encourage the religious viewpoints of those who will attempt to subvert liberal standards of academic discourse and civility.[2]

Fish's extreme view of how religious belief must subvert liberalism is particularly welcome because it provides an opportunity to explain where such reasoning goes wrong. While it is certainly true that some religious believers wish to destroy the pluralistic academy, there are many other religious viewpoints, including some theologically conservative ones, which harbor no such desire. It is perfectly possible, for instance, to hold, as I do, an Augustinian view that faith in God, rather than faith in self or material contingency, should shape one's essential vision of reality and yet to support the rules of liberal society as a God-given means for accomplishing some limited but immensely valuable goals.

Nor am I, as I have emphasized, advocating a sort of postmodernism in which, because precommitments condition reason, "anything goes." Rather, the problem as I see it is how to balance the advocacy implicit in all scholarship with academic standards that are scientific or "reasonable" in the sense of being accessible to people from many different ideological camps. Traditional religious viewpoints, I am saying, can be just as hospitable to scientifically sound investigation as many other viewpoints, all of which are ultimately grounded in some faith or other. Hence religious perspectives ought to be recognized as legitimate in the mainstream academy so long as their proponents are willing to support the rules necessary for constructive exchange of ideas in a pluralistic setting.

## THE VALUE OF THE LIBERAL
## PRAGMATIC ACADEMY

William James, in his famous essay "What Pragmatism Means," provides a helpful image of how a liberal pluralistic society ought to work. James describes pragmatic liberal discourse as like a corridor in a hotel. Innumerable chambers open out of it. In one you may find a man writing an atheistic volume; in the next someone on his knees praying for faith and strength; in the third a chemist investigating a body's properties. In a fourth a system of idealistic metaphysics is being excogitated; in a fifth the impossibility of metaphysics is being shown. But they all own the corridor, and all must pass through it if they want a practicable way of getting into or out of their respective rooms.[3]

I find this image quite congenial. Essentially my position is that in a pluralistic society we have little choice but to accept pragmatic standards in public life. I am not, as some might suppose, challenging pragmatic liberalism as the modus operandi for the contemporary academy.[4] Rather I am affirming it for that limited role, but arguing that there is no adequate pragmatic basis for marginalizing all supernaturalist religious viewpoints a priori. There is no basic reason why the intellectual implications of particular religious beliefs may not be explicitly brought into public discourse. I would be happy, in fact, if someone like William James were in charge of setting the rules for these corridors, as I think he would have appreciated this point.

What I am wary of, however, is of having the spiritual descendants of John Dewey in charge. The tendency of twentieth-century liberal culture has been to absolutize the pragmatic method. The absolute, that value than which there is none higher, is that which promotes civil discourse. Virtues such as tolerance, openness, dialogue, agnosticism, mutuality, equal opportunity, scientific method, truth-seeking, charity, and love of beauty might be on a list of "the top ten" commandments. John Dewey recognized the potential religious functions of such a liberal polity and even attempted to promote it as "a common faith."[5] So absolutized, liberal pragmatism has little tolerance for traditionalist religions that challenge the pragmatic absolutes.

If, however, pragmatism (and liberal polity generally) is recognized as not an absolute, but simply as a relatively good method for dealing peacefully and with equity among diverse peoples, then those for whom the public domain is not ultimate can readily support it as they should support any relative good.

*Christian Scholarship and the Rules of the Academic Game*

Is there something peculiar, though, about self-consciously Christian scholars that make them particularly likely to violate the essential canons of scientific investigation of the mainstream academy? Regarding most of the technical scholarship that makes up the vast majority of academic inquiry, there is no reason to expect such a difference. In the corridors of the pragmatic academy Christians and non-Christians can readily share basic standards of evidence and argument. These standards work in separating good arguments from bad, and on many topics they can establish a sort of "public knowledge" that persons from many ideological sub-communities can agree on and which are not simply matters of opinion. Christians and non-Christians likely will use precisely the same methods in determining the date when George Washington crossed the Delaware to attack the Hessians at Trenton. There is no reason why persons of conventional religious convictions might not be thoroughly expert at employing the scientific academic conventions that lead to the establishment of such widely attested beliefs.[6] The issue here is not essentially different from that of whether a conventional Christian might not be an excellent private detective, as G. K. Chesterton and his character, "Father Brown," were among the first to illustrate.

The fact is that explicitly Christian convictions do not very often have substantial impact on the techniques used in academic detective work, which make up the bulk of the technical, scientific side of academic inquiry. Christians, just as other scholars, must employ the requisite degree of detachment in order to weigh evidence judiciously. And even though they may be passionately motivated to do the best job of truth-seeking, they must be duly dispassionate in order to think clearly and to present their results effectively, without tendentiousness.

It might be objected, however, that if Christian scholarship involves anything that makes it distinctive beyond such technical knowledge, it will violate rules essential to the mainstream academy in just those respects. What would make it distinctively Christian is likely to depend on claims of revelation, or sources of knowledge not shared by others. Hence it would violate rules essential for promoting fruitful public discourse. This is a somewhat different objection from that dealt with in the previous chapter, that all knowledge in the academy must be empirically verifiable. As we have seen, such a rule would exclude far too many beliefs that academics hold dear. The present concern is more analogous to the problem of introducing special revelations into a court of law. It simply does not advance the discussion to argue on the basis of an authority that some people regard as supreme and others regard as bogus.

This seems to be a valid concern as far as it goes. In a pluralistic public setting it makes sense to have a rule that representatives of various religious beliefs not argue on the basis of the authority of their special or private revelations. It simply does not advance the discussion to introduce an authority that other people do not accept.

## SCHOLARSHIP THAT IS SHAPED BY BACKGROUND RELIGIOUS COMMITMENTS

There is, however, another category of scholarship that relates revelatory claims to one's research but which should not be objectionable. One's worldview may be fundamentally shaped by beliefs that ultimately rest on claims to revelation or other sources of authority not shared by most people. For instance, one might believe that all warfare is wrong because it violates a command of Jesus. Or one might think that Jesus' commands dictate that one should take a stand for racial justice or care for the poor. Others might hold that God's revelation shows that humans are naturally corrupt and that one should be suspicious of utopian hopes that presume a general improvement in human behavior. Still others may believe, on the contrary, that revelation shows that there is hope for a general improvement in human behavior.

Any of these viewpoints might be introduced into the mainstream academy for religious reasons, but defended with arguments and evidence that are publicly accessible. The approach would be equivalent to Catholic natural law arguments. Secularists themselves would not have to believe in the principle of a God-given natural law in order to accept arguments based on widely held beliefs. So their having a religious *source* does not automatically exclude one's views from acceptance in the academy so long as one argues for them on other, more widely accessible, grounds.

In practice, however, the academy does not work on such a consistently rational basis. Most history departments would be more uncomfortable with a fundamentalist dispensationalist (who believed that God had ordained a special role for Israel in the end times) teaching modern diplomatic history than they would with a deeply religious Jew who saw comparable significance in the Israeli cause.[7] It is hard to see why there should not be room for both as long as their work is of a high quality and can be evaluated by the usual standards. Nonetheless, examples such as this point out that there may be special prejudices against certain views. Consider, for instance, someone whose religious beliefs lead her to maintain that abortion is a kind of murder, or that homosexual relationships are sinful. Whatever the source of such beliefs, there is going to be strong resistance to relating them to one's scholarship in the mainstream academy. Sometimes the reason given for such resistance will be that people should not let their religious prejudices intrude into their scholarship. That argument, however, is a red herring since it is not consistently applied. Indeed, there is no way that it could be applied without excluding too much. No one, for example, is going to rule out of bounds for the mainstream academy the views of a pious liberal Episcopalian psychologist who holds that homosexual relationships may be important to human fulfillment, even though that view may ultimately have a religious origin. On the other hand, the views of an equally competent but very conservative Episcopalian psychologist who argued that homosexual relationships are likely to be destructive would be much more likely to be dismissed as illicitly religious in origin.[8]

One should also notice that the operative rules in the pragmatic academy do not exclude all background beliefs or authorities that are not shared by most academics. Any such rule would, like the rule that all beliefs must be empirically verifiable, exclude far too many beliefs. For instance, such a rule would exclude many minority opinions on moral issues. Before they became widespread, beliefs such as that slavery is wrong or that women and men are equal would have been ruled out because they were based on authority of moral principles that were self-evident only to some people.

It seems to follow, then, that minority religious beliefs, like minority moral beliefs, should be permissible as background beliefs in the academy. As background beliefs, these are not ideas that we would normally introduce into the pragmatic academy as the *evidence* for our views. For that we would look to other beliefs that we share with persons from differing ideological camps, so that we could argue on common grounds. Some of the Quakers who early opposed slavery may have done so for primarily religious reasons, but they argued their case in Enlightenment terms of equality. Today, as then, religious people might argue their cases by pointing out some internal inconsistencies in the belief systems of others. They might point out, for instance, that contemporary academic dogmatism on questions of equality and justice is inconsistent with the affirmation of purely naturalist Darwinism. They would thus be arguing their case on grounds that could be widely shared.

Despite the fact that we do not articulate some of our background beliefs as evidence or arguments in pluralistic academic settings, they may still play a significant role. Nicholas Wolterstorff refers to these significant background beliefs as "control beliefs."[9] Such beliefs, even if not directly expressed, act as significant controls on what other beliefs and theories we are willing to entertain. The presence of these beliefs in our web of beliefs may also affect the relative importance that we assign to other beliefs that we hold.

It is, of course, fair game in academia to smoke out and to attack the background control beliefs that account for a fellow academic's dogmatism. If I can show that a colleague's controversial opinions are grounded in a blind allegiance to racism, Marxism, liberalism, humanism, anything French and obscure, or to a religious dogma, I may have a reason to be suspicious of her views.

Nonetheless, in cases of allegiance to ideologies such as those just mentioned, the love for one's basic commitments is not necessarily blind. On the one hand, each of these views rests on foundations that are ultimately mysterious, rather than scientific. So do liberal pragmatic views. On the other hand, there are versions of each of these viewpoints that are carefully reasoned and weighed against other sources of knowledge and which can be shown to rest on no shakier ground than do some of the most widely accepted views in the academy. If representatives of such views, including religiously based views, are willing to play by the other rules of the academy, there seems no reason why their views should be discredited just because they involve some background dogmatism.

If the main point of this line of argument, then, is to say that religious beliefs might legitimately serve as important background control beliefs for tamed academics in the mainstream academy, it might be asked what the fuss is about. Such modestly held beliefs do already form the background for the work of many academics. There is little evidence of prejudice against scholars who happen to have such religious views. So what really is at stake?

MAKING RELIGIOUS PERSPECTIVES EXPLICIT

What is at stake is whether religious scholars should be virtually required to keep their religious views hidden. Should religious views be put in a special category of "personal beliefs" that scholars are not encouraged to think seriously about? Would only the self-indulgent reveal those thoughts in public?

Thomas Bender, a leading American intellectual historian, in a thoughtful review of *The Soul of the American University*, puts the case for the academic privatization of religious belief this way:

> The privatization of belief is not the same as its dissolution. Our private beliefs are not diminished by being disestablished. They are relocated and shorn of formal authority, but they are not isolated from public culture. As our daily experience reveals, private beliefs contribute to the making of a particular thinking self that offers an individual and distinctive contribution to the public discussion of scholarship.

Bender goes on to argue that there is not much evidence of prejudice against religious belief in academia because in fact many academics are personally religious and their religious views inevitably bear on their academic work.[10]

Bender goes beyond many observers in his recognition of the legitimacy of religious perspectives implicitly shaping scholarship. Yet one has to wonder about his conclusion that implicit influences are sufficient and not a diminishment. If religious beliefs are relevant to understanding one's other beliefs, it seems as though it would be valuable in a pluralistic setting to reflect openly on that considerable dimension in one's intellectual makeup. Otherwise the intellectual implications of one's beliefs are less likely to be rigorously developed. One would not likely say to feminists, Marxists, neoconservatives, gay advocates, and representatives of other viewpoints that the privatization of their viewpoints would not be a diminishment. The question, as I see it, is whether there is a compelling reason why all religious viewpoints should be placed in the private category.

It is worth repeating that what we are talking about is largely a matter of self-censorship. Younger scholars who are Christian quickly learn that influential professors hold negative attitudes toward open religious expression and that to be accepted they should keep quiet about their faith. So rather than attempting to reflect on the relationship between religious faith and their other beliefs, they learn to hide their religious beliefs in professional settings. Such self-censorship by its very nature proceeds quietly, but the attitudes it fosters are pervasive.

It is essential to reiterate that the alternative being proposed is that there be room for explict Christian points of view (just as there are explicit Marxist or feminist views) for those who will play by the other rules proper to the diverse academy. Most often when people rule out religious perspectives they miss this latter qualification. They assume that the proposal involves opening the academy to all sorts of additional ideological dogmatism and preaching that would cut off intellectual exchange rather than promote it. As I have emphasized, that is a danger with any strongly held position and it is always a struggle to keep some partisans within the bounds of fair discourse and argument. Recognizing that, I am simply proposing that the same rules apply to all. No matter what commitments one brings into one's academic work, one would have to argue for one's scholarly interpretations on the same sorts of publicly accessible grounds that are widely accepted in the academy. I have already argued this point with respect to background beliefs. I am now proposing only the addition of granting that scholars are not transgressing the integrity of public intellectual life if they occasionally identify or reflect upon the religious sources of their views. In many cases I think that would be helpful to others in the academy in aiding them in understanding the roots of one's position.

Even though religious people should honor the rule that they cannot offer their special revelations as the public evidence for their views, they can still reflect on the implications of such revelations within the bounds of the mainstream academy by talking about them conditionally. That is, it is perfectly legitimate to ask an academic question in the form of "if this religious teaching were true, how would it change the way we look at the subject at hand?" Some versions of that question may not interest most scholars. For instance, if one asked what difference it would make if it were true, as most of the major religions claim, that the universe is a product of an intelligence, it would have a major bearing on many topics. We shall discuss those differences in the next chapters. For the moment, however, the point is that the mainstream academy typically operates only on the basis of the opposite conditional statement. It operates on the basis of the conditional "if we assume there is no creator god, what sense can we make out of reality?"

While debates over such fundamental issues should not be excluded from the mainstream academy, they have to be conducted with a degree of restraint that is sometimes difficult to delimit precisely. For instance, one of the rules for religious people, as for other committed scholars working within the mainstream academy, is that they must not be simply proselytizing. Since proselytizing is so central to many religious movements and since many people adamantly oppose anything that might be construed as state promotion of religion, this issue is one to which religious scholars should be especially sensitive. It is, of course, difficult to avoid trying to persuade others of the merits of one's own views. Christians can and should be allowed to explain and defend their own viewpoints and, in the proper settings, attempt to persuade others of their superiority, just as advocates of feminist, Marxist, liberal democratic, neoconservative, or purely naturalistic views often do. In classrooms, especially in state-supported schools, teachers must present such viewpoints only as relevant to the academic subject and with great deference and respect for opposing viewpoints, especially opposing religious views. Discourse on religious topics in the pluralistic academy must be conducted with willingness to listen as well as to speak. Such standards of civility are not always respected by nonreligious scholars in the current academy, but they nevertheless represent a moral ideal that religious scholars should be conspicuous in supporting. Otherwise academia will be reduced to a sort of Hyde Park Corner where every evangelist or ideologue has his own soapbox.

The rule that religious scholars should follow here is, I think, some version of the golden rule. How would we want scholars holding other strongly ideological convictions to act in the mainstream academy? Traditional Christians, for instance, might ask how they would want Mormon scholars to act, or Marxist scholars, or feminist scholars. They should not argue that just because some other groups violate the rules for civil discourse, Christians should as well. Rather, Christians should be models of what it means to love and respect those with whom one differs, even as they may debate their differences.

It is, I think, the analogy of religious scholarship to feminist, Marxist, African-American, or gay advocacy scholarship that leads many liberal scholars to be wary of opening the doors to religious perspectives. They assume that what we are proposing is the admission of all sorts of additional brands of tendentious scholarship. That is, of course, a danger, but I can only repeat that this is not what I am proposing. I do not favor tendentious scholarship, whether it comes from religious scholars, advocates of multiculturalism, or liberals. All these groups are prone to tendentiousness, but in none of them is it necessary to their scholarship.

My own view is that scholarship that is simply tendentious is in the long run self-defeating. Often it has an impact in the short run, enlisting thinkers who are willing to substitute formulae for original thought. Champions of such scholarly causes can gain considerable political power. In the long run, however, they lose their credibility. Their views become drearily predictable, and other scholars cease to take them seriously. Nonetheless, even if some scholarship in the academy inevitably is tendentious, it is better that the sources of the tendentiousness be identified so that they can be the more easily discounted. The convention of insisting that all scholars and teachers pose as disinterested observers is more misleading than a general rule of frank identification of one's biases.

A more mature version of ideologically oriented scholarship will include criticism of its own tradition, rather than a simple celebration of everyone and everything that is on one's side. Christian scholarship ought especially to be marked by such traits. Christians, after all, are taught to be critical about their own saints, as the Bible abundantly illustrates. Those who take seriously that salvation is by God's grace should not be surprised to find all sorts of failings even among the best of Christians and their institutions. Ideally, then, Christian scholarship should provide a refreshing alternative to the sorts of partisanship that mark the outlooks of many communities.

My ideal for Christian scholarship is one that not only looks for the bearing of one's Christian convictions on one's academic thought, but also reflects some Christian attitudes that shape the tone of one's scholarship.

Not only should Christian commitments lead one toward scholarly rigor and integrity, they should also encourage fairness and charity toward those with whom one differs. Representatives of many other religious traditions would say the same thing. Scholarship with these qualities will ultimately have the greatest impact in the academy and the greatest chance of being accepted.

## CHRISTIAN SCHIZOPHRENIA?

Finally, we come back to the objection raised by Stanley Fish, an objection also heard from some strongly religious people. Have we not conceded too much, they ask, in order to get a hearing in the mainstream academy for no more than occasional discussions of the implications of such broad frames of reference? Are we not saying, in effect, that one has to water down religious faith and witness so that it will be acceptable to the diverse pragmatic academy? Does that not make a religious person schizophrenic, advocating and perhaps proselytizing for a life-changing worldview in one part of his life, but playing by rules that are not consistently Christian the rest of the time? Are we not saying in effect that on one day a week we say, "Choose you this day whom you will serve," and on the other six we serve the rules of the pragmatic academy?

Here I think the answer is that it is in the very nature of human life that every day we routinely move from one field of activity to another, each with its own set of rules. Such adaptability to the subordinate communities in which a Christian may operate is fully consistent with Christian commitment. It is the principle, I think, behind the saying of Jesus that we should "render unto Caesar the things that are Caesar's." It is also the fundamental principle of Augustine's *City of God* which posits that, although our primary allegiance is to the City of God, we also have subordinate and limited allegiances to human governments, which necessarily run on sub-Christian principles. We should think of ourselves as "resident aliens," as some of my friends say, but as resident aliens we should obey the laws of the land of our sojourn to the extent that they do not conflict with our higher allegiances.[11]

I think it is helpful to view these adaptations to the rules of various institutions of the larger society as analogous to games that religious people may play. Christians often spend hours playing by the rules of basketball, for example. Literally applying the ethics of Jesus, passing the ball equally to your opponents as much as to your teammates, would not do much for the game. Or try playing chess with someone who does not want to gain at the expense of his neighbor. In fact in the game situation the best way to show love to your opponent is to play fairly by the competitive rules of the game. So when religious people play by the rules of the various games of society—the rules of law, the pragmatic rules of the United States Constitution, the rules of the market, or the rules of mainstream academia—they are not necessarily violating Christian principles by temporarily accommodating themselves to those rules.

At the same time, there are limits to one's allegiance to such rules. Christians cannot play some of the games of society and they cannot accept some of the prevailing rules of other games. Nonetheless, there are many social conventions to which Christians can give limited allegiance. When engaged in such activities, the situation of the religious believer may be analogous to a doctor who is playing softball. So long as she is in the softball game, she tries not to break its rules. If, however, she sees a car accident on a nearby street, she will stop running the bases and go to help. The rules of doctoring take precedence over baseball rules.

So with religious people in the academy. They are free to play by the academy's rules to the extent that these do not conflict directly with their Christian commitments. As I said earlier, many of the pragmatic rules for getting along with our diverse neighbors and even with our enemies are the sorts of rules that Christians should readily adopt for such limited, though important, purposes. They are, like civil government, ordained by God to keep the peace and should be valued accordingly.

Some of the rules for getting along equitably in a pluralistic academic situation are different from the rules within the Christian church, but not contradictory to them. So what may be appropriate to a church gathering may not be appropriate to an academic gathering. Preaching sermons and public prayer are not appropriate to teaching in state universities or speaking to a session of the American Historical Association. The Body of Christ, however, has many members, and Christians may have many callings. That means not only that some Christians are called to one task and others to another, but also that each Christian may be called to work in differing settings at different times. Some scholars may be called to serve strictly in the church and in its schools. Such academic communities are invaluable and can sustain a depth of sophistication regarding the implications of faith and scholarship that is unattainable in diverse settings. Nonetheless most Christian scholars today have good reason also to be participating in pluralistic enterprises such as mainstream scholarship. In such settings it would be self-defeating to insist that the only rules one will follow are those that would be appropriate to the church. When one wants to speak to diverse audiences, one must be willing to accommodate to the language and rules designed for that community—to be all things to all people. As one Christian scholar remarked to me, "when in Rome, do as the Romans do. When in academia, use academic conventions."

## SO HOW OUTRAGEOUS IS IT?

What has been said so far could be read as sending two conflicting messages. One, as argued in the first two chapters, is that there is a longstanding and deeply seated antagonism between the modern academy and the more traditional forms of Christianity. The other message, suggested in this chapter, is that even very traditional Christian perspectives need not be so outrageous after all, but can fit in nicely with the current rules of the academy if only those rules are applied equally to religious and nonreligious views.

Both these points are true and each needs to qualify the other. Christians must remember that, much as they may value liberal institutions, they are participating in them on an ad hoc basis, limited by higher allegiances. They must keep in mind that ultimately there is an inherent "offense" in the Gospel and so there will be deep underlying mutual opposition in relation to some other points of view. At the root of that opposition is the question of highest allegiance. Christians have been and should be critical of some of the assumptions on which liberal academic culture has been built and it is not surprising that the favor is returned. The same applies to the relationships between Christianity and other currently popular academic ideologies. Even when Christians are sympathetic to them, they are likely to give them only limited allegiance. So, as Stanley Fish has suggested, we cannot solve the problems of religion and public life by saying, "Why can't we all just get along?"[12] Ultimately we do not solve all the problems of pluralism by better communication and more "dia-logue." The more we understand each other the more likely we are to also discover some fundamental differences.

That being said, there is nothing wrong and a lot right with trying to get along better, and that is one of the things that the rules of the liberal academy help us do. Deeply religious people should be participating fully in that academy and they should be working to improve its rules, particularly those that tend to marginalize their own views. The rules of the academy are not fixed or inevitable. They are constantly evolving and as they do they may not be self-consistent. Religious people should point out those inconsistencies and suggest how the rules might be improved.

It may even be, as some people will argue, that if religious people observe all the other requisite rules of the academy they will find little prejudice against explicitly religious views. I suspect this is often true. One should not underestimate the legacy of historical antagonism between some elements in the modern academy and traditional Christianity, but there is no doubt that some proponents of various Christian orthodoxies have always been highly regarded in the mainstream academy. So there is no hard and fast rule against relating faith to learning. That may be all the more reason, however, to ask why so few scholars in mainstream academic settings work to relate their deeply held religious commitments to their intellectual lives.

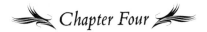 *Chapter Four*

# What Difference Could It Possibly Make?

Having affirmed that Christian perspectives need not subvert the essential standards of the mainstream academy, Christian scholars are likely to be confronted with the opposite sort of objection. If Christian academics are as tamed as I have described—if they are not quoting Bible verses or claiming to read God's providence—what difference could Christian scholarship possibly make?

The next two chapters explore this issue. This chapter responds to some of the most significant questions that are likely to be raised regarding the possibility or advisability of developing identifiably Christian scholarship. It also sketches some of the *types* of ways in which we should expect Christian perspectives to have real impact. The next chapter builds on that base to suggest how some central Christian theological affirmations might reshape some of our other academic thought.

Many thoughtful people, including many Christians, are simply puzzled at the suggestion that, if scholarship measures up to the other usual standards of the mainstream academy, Christianity should make it somehow different. Here, for instance, is one of the more passionately stated versions of this frequently heard objection:

> It is hard to believe that Marsden actually means what he says, and it occurs to me that he has not thought through clearly the claims that he makes. Does he think that at his university, Notre Dame, they teach

a Roman Catholic chemistry? Or that Aryan biology would be sanctioned at his former university, Duke?

This carries over into the social sciences and history as well. Would Calvin College actually devote itself to Presbyterian anthropology or worry that Episcopal psychology should get a hearing? Should historians of the Reformation be primarily identified as Protestant, French, or female? As I have said, there are serious issues to be confronted here. But the perspectivalism that Marsden appears to defend demeans his vision of the university.[1]

This is a helpful passage because it states so forcefully the most common line of argument against the very idea of Christian perspectives. The argument is that there are lots of academic topics which Christian perspectives, or in this case denominational perspectives, do not seem to change substantially. Hence it seems that we must be chasing a phantom.

Yet even the examples from this very strong version of the point do not self-evidently lead to that conclusion. For instance, the question of whether the primary identification for historians of the Reformation might be Protestant, French, or female is one on which there is much current debate. Certainly many would think that a *relevant* identification for historians of the Reformation would be whether they are Protestant or female. Even knowing that an historian is French may be a clue that we are in for some heavy weather on the interpretive front.

Even some denominational differences can have relevance to interpretation. It is easy to see how there might be (in fact there is) a Mennonite view of political science or a Roman Catholic view of nuclear war, labor and capital, or medical ethics (all subjects of recent pronouncements of Catholic bishops or the Pope). In fact, conservative Presbyterians and other Reformed Christians, such as those at Calvin College, *do* have a view of human nature (and hence of anthropology in both its classic and modern senses) that distinguishes their outlook from the more optimistic views of many other Christians and secularists. One would not call this the *Presbyterian* view, since some Presbyterians do not believe in "total depravity," while many non-Presbyterians do believe in it, but such a belief does have relevance to many scholarly interpretations.

For those of us who have been part of a Christian scholarly community such as Calvin College the suggestion that faith-informed perspectives do not make a real difference to scholarship is as puzzling as is the contrary for some critics.[2] In such academic communities there is constant alertness to Christian perspectives and what differences they may or may not make.[3] Everyone recognizes that the differences will not be apparent in the technical dimensions of their work, but that implications of the faith may sometimes have an important bearing on their theories and interpretations. Even mathematicians or technical scientists will be able to point out some faith-related considerations that have relevance to the foundational questions affecting the frameworks of their disciplines or the applications of their work. It simply does not follow that, because there is no special Christian view of photosynthesis, there is therefore not a Christian view of biology.

I find that a helpful image for explaining the apparently elusive idea that there can be both many commonalities and important differences between Christian and non-Christian scholarship is that of a gestalt picture, like the one that seen one way looks like a duck, but viewed another way seems to be a rabbit. Gestalt images fit well with prevailing descriptions of how the human mind works. We organize experience according to available patterns that the mind has at its disposal. To some extent the patterns that we use to organize our perceptions seem to be nearly universal among humans. We can all perceive individual trees in the midst of the massive influx of data that we receive when we look into a forest. Other patterns, or aspects of patterns, are culturally conditioned. A premodern person who looked into an airplane cockpit would see a bewildering assortment of

Duck or Rabbit?

shapes and lights. Most of us might see only a control board pattern. An experienced pilot might perceive a entire flight situation and a possible emergency shaping up.

As the gestalt images suggest, our perception of these patterns is based not on a logical deduction from sorting through all the data (the way a computer might process it), but rather from a few clues that trigger the whole pattern. It also illustrates how different people can perceive completely different overall patterns, even while each is looking at identical data. Almost all of our experience is organized in this holistic way.

This model of how we perceive helps us understand the similarities and differences between Christian and non-Christian scholarship. To the extent that we deal with many aspects of individual "facts," our scholarship will be identical. If we are measuring, for instance, the ratio of black to white in the duck/rabbit picture, we will use identical procedures and, with the proper definitions, come to conclusions with which everyone can agree. At higher levels of interpretation, however, we might differ radically on the overall meaning or relative importance of the facts. What is a bill for those who see the duck pattern are the ears for the rabbit school of thought.

In contemporary scholarship, we see comparable patterns of similarity and difference all the time. Two scholars might be able to agree perfectly on the details of the Battle of Little Bighorn—where and when it took place, how many people were killed on both sides, even (perhaps) who fired the first shot. What they can plausibly say is limited by the evidence. Nonetheless, one scholar might see the battle as Custer's heroic last stand in a fight to bring peace to the American West; another might see it as a triumph in the Native American fight to resist barbaric invaders. While at one level such differences might look like mere partisanship, at a deeper level they have to do with large-scale beliefs about what the world is, or should be, like.

As we have observed, background beliefs will have a vast influence on which pattern we see when we look at "the facts." Perhaps we can more clearly see how this works if we go beyond the somewhat limited analogy of the gestalt picture and think of the pictures as including some revealing clues that are colored in such a way as to be visible only when wearing a certain set of glasses. Again there are good analogies to common academic controversies. As long as most Americans looked at the relationships of whites to Indians only through the lenses of nationalism, scholars seldom saw the Indian wars from Native American perspectives. Once moral sensitivities to the oppression of minorities became widespread, a new generation of scholars saw the same information through a new set of glasses. The evidence had not changed, but now the advance of the white settlements of America was more often understood as an "invasion."

Often, the interpretive differences are not so dramatic, however, thus helping to account for why some scholars fail to see them. Serious religious beliefs help shape not only our overt ways of valuing things, but also our priorities. What do we see as important to study? What is it about that subject which makes it interesting? What are the questions we ask that will organize our interpretations of this topic? What theories do we entertain as relevant to our interpretations? What theories do we rule out?

## SCHOLARLY AGENDAS

The broadest way that Christianity, or any other religious faith, makes a difference to scholarship, then, is in the scholarly agendas that faith will help set. As the discussion of the duck/rabbit gestalt image suggests, the degree that the relevance of the faith will be apparent will vary greatly with the topic. The more amenable a problem is to tightly controlled empirical observation, the less the apparent relevance. Yet as any topic, including empirical investigation, touches on questions of wider significance or meaning, faith becomes more obviously relevant. So on topics that have the most to do with interpretation and with the larger significance and meaning of humans in relation to each other and the universe, faith-related perspectives will have the most bearing. Such implications are more often apparent in the humanities and social sciences than in the hard sciences. Philosophers are likely more often to be able to identify the pertinence of religious perspectives for their work than will historians or social scientists, who in turn will be able to point to religious influences more often than will chemists or physicists.

Nonetheless, even in largely technical disciplines religious faith can have an important bearing on scholarship in at least four ways. First, it may be a factor in motivating a scholar to do her work well. That is not to say that nonreligious scholars may not be just as motivated to work with just as much integrity. For any particular scholar, however, religious faith may be an important motivator. Second, religious faith may help determine the applications one sees for his scholarship. One may do technical work in anything from epidemiology to engineering with the hope that it may contribute to the well-being of others. Again, that many nonreligious people are also altruistic does not negate the religious contribution to altruism. Third, such motives may help shape a sub-field, specialty, or questions one asks about one's work. Fourth, when on occasion the technical scholar is asked to reflect on the wider implications of her scholarship, faith may have an important bearing on how she sees the field, or its assumptions, fitting into a larger framework of meaning.

As one comes to disciplines that deal with interpretations about humans and their relationships to the world and to others, the last two of these four factors rise in relative significance. As we have seen in the discussion of background beliefs, such significance is not always explicit, obvious, or uniquely Christian. It is there, nonetheless, shaping the very topics on which scholars choose to work. One commentator, attempting to undercut the analogy between Christian perspectives and feminist perspectives, asked "whether Christianity is generating a number of exciting new research programs, as feminism has proved able to do."[4] His implication was that Christian scholars were not producing such work. In fact, they are. Christian motives often determine what fields people go into, what topics they study in those fields, and what questions they ask about those topics. The big difference from feminism is that the Christian factors that shape such agendas are largely kept secret and underground. Often the scholars themselves have not reflected much on the influence.

The most obvious manifestation of Christianity shaping research agendas is in direct examination of the cultural roles of Christianity itself. Christian scholars will often ask questions about how Christian beliefs influenced or were influenced by some other dimensions of human behavior. Much of the work of Christians in the field of literature has been of this sort. Many literary studies have been written about how Christian themes have been manifested in the works of various writers, and often these studies grow out of the scholar's own religious commitments. In my own field of history there are a number of striking examples of such fruitful agendas, for instance, Charles Hambrick-Stowe's *The Practice of Piety,* a wonderfully crafted and highly admired account of Puritan piety.

Only a Christian, I think, is likely to take questions about piety as seriously on their own terms as Hambrick-Stowe does. Nathan Hatch's much acclaimed *Democratization of American Religion* is built on insights arising from decades of an insider's reflections on the relationship of evangelicalism to democratic culture. Dale Van Kley's ground-breaking studies of the religious origins of the French Revolution have offered much discussed challenges to interpretations that offered only secular explanations for an event that had notoriously secularizing results.[5] Once again an insider's sensibilities to both the force and the ambiguities of religious influences were pivotal to a creative research agenda.

Christian influence on scholarship is not confined, however, to the study of Christianity itself. As is true of any tradition of thought, it involves a characteristic set of questions and larger perspectives which, while not always taking formal shape, permeate inquiry in many subtle ways. Robert Wuthnow, a Christian and a distinguished sociologist, has referred to this effect as "living the question." He writes:

> I have borrowed the much-used phrase "living the question" because it seems to me that Christianity does not so much supply the learned person with answers as it does raise questions. It has been said of Marxists that even apostates spend their lives struggling with the questions Marx addressed. The same can probably be said of Christianity. It leaves people with a set of questions they cannot escape, especially when these questions face them from their earliest years.

Wuthnow explains further:

> The particular questions are likely to vary. What Christianity does is add seriousness to the enterprise: it says, in effect, these are serious questions that people have raised in one way or another from the beginning of time; do your part to keep them alive. . . .
>
> Putting it differently, we might say that Christianity *sacralizes*—makes sacred—the intellectual life. It gives the questions we struggle with in our work and in our lives a larger significance.[6]

These are important points about the subtle but pervasive influences of faith on a Christian's scholarship.

## BUT SHOULD WE MAKE A POINT OF IT?

Wuthnow also raises some of the most serious insider questions about Christian scholarship. For all his affirmation of these differences, he is reluctant to go beyond these subtleties. In the essay just quoted, he is willing to identify himself as a Christian, but he also makes clear that such openness is by far to be the exception rather than the rule. Wuthnow spells out these reservations in a review of Mark Noll's much-discussed *The Scandal of the Evangelical Mind*.[7] Noll, whose agenda resembes mine, calls on evangelical Christians to develop more credible Christian scholarship. Wuthnow puts his reservations this way:

> On the one hand, he [Noll] argues that evangelical Christians should be addressing their disciplines from a distinct Christian framework that privileges Christian assumptions about human nature, God, Christ, redemption, and eschatology. On the other hand, he seems to be suggesting that the best scholarship is done by people who simply take the created order seriously enough to study it with as much care as anyone else. I am more in sympathy with the second view than with the first. . . . The harder task is to take one's subject matter seriously enough to understand it from many different perspectives. For if that is the goal, then good Christian scholarship may be virtually indistinguishable from scholarship done by anyone else. In my own discipline of sociology, for instance, studies of impoverished families, community service, personal morality, health reform, sexuality, and values have flourished in recent years—much of it is compatible with a Christian worldview, and yet little of it flaunts that perspective.[8]

This passage is worth quoting at length because it comes from a serious Christian whose scholarship is renowned for its judiciousness. If someone who is so sympathetic to the cause of Christian scholarship believes that the best such scholarship may be indistinguishable from non-Christian scholarship, one cannot write it off as the result of prejudice.[9]

One important dimension of Wuthnow's critique is his choice of the term "flaunts" to describe making Christian views explicit. Clearly he and some other Christian scholars find it embarrassing, in bad taste, or perhaps just a little pretentious to have scholars trying to identify the "Christian" view of this or that. It may be perceived as claiming divine sanction for one's point of view, or as claiming that one's scholarship is automatically superior to the scholarship of others. Perhaps most seriously in many academic circles, if you say your scholarship is "Christian," people will immediately ask whether that means that it is opposed to that of other religions. Is it anti-Jewish, for example?

These legitimate issues suggest that the question of identifying one's work as "Christian" should be handled with discretion. In many pluralistic settings it would not be something to which one would call attention. When one does, as was suggested in the introduction, it might be best to refer to one's scholarship with the more modest "faith-informed," while readily identifying oneself as a Christian. Graduate students, for instance, are usually best advised to master their disciplines and the art of communicating with diverse audiences before parading their "Christian" critiques which are supposed to revolutionize the field. On the other hand, a Christian perspective should not be treated as a dark secret to be suppressed. Rather, one ought to be cultivating it and reflecting upon it as part of one's scholarly identity, and it should be a proper part of occasional scholarly self-disclosure—a modest way of saying, "This is where my scholarship is coming from," or "Many of my background beliefs are shaped by my Christianity and I am attempting to understand what implications they may have for my scholarship."

Thus occasionally identifying Christian sources in one's thought is quite different from claiming that it represents *the* Christian view and hence by virtue of divine sanction trumps all other views. Of course, all scholars should be aiming at discovering and defending the truth as best they can, and need not pretend that they think all points of view are equal. But as Wuthnow argues (in his own exemplary Christian way), the best scholarship sympathetically sees what the subject looks like from numerous perspectives. It can therefore set a tone of such fairness as to obviate accusations that one is operating from a biased viewpoint. Certainly Wuthnow's own scholarship is much admired for displaying just such traits.

If one sets up as a standard for Christian scholarship something like such Wuthnovian fair-mindedness, as opposed to flaunting Christian perspectives or using them as substitutes for sound scholarship, then his position overlaps substantially with Noll's and mine. As his list of examples of topics of recent sociological study that fit with Christian perspectives suggests, Wuthnow recognizes that the questions Christians ask have substantial bearing on their work, and this influence goes beyond just adding serious-ness (although that is the only point he emphasizes). Christian perspectives help determine both the very topics that scholars study and questions they will ask about those topics. Wuthnow prefers to play down the substantive influences of Christian commitments, while I want to encourage more open reflection on their intellectual implications. Nonetheless, if one looks at just the titles of some of Wuthnow's own recent works, the marks of substantive Christian concerns are evident, even if their fair-minded tone makes them seem indistinguishable from what a non-Christian might write. These titles include: *The Restructuring of American Religion* (1988), *The Struggle for America's Soul: Evangelicals, Liberals, and Secularism* (1989), *Communities of Discourse: Ideology and Social Structure in the Reformation, the Enlightenment, and European Socialism* (1989), *Faith and Philanthropy* (1990), *Rediscovering the Sacred: Perspectives on Religion in Contemporary Society* (1992), *Christianity in the Twenty-First Century: Reflections on the Challenges Ahead* (1993), *God and Mammon in America* (1994), *Sharing the Journey: Support Groups and America's New Quest for Community* (1994), and *Learning to Care: Elementary Kindness in an Age of Indifference* (1995).

## IS IT DISTINCTIVE?

Is there, however, anything *distinctively* Christian in all this? Christians sometimes talk about "distinct Christian principles" shaping scholarship. Yet there is no reason in principle why a person of another faith or of no formal faith might not come up with these same topics.[10] Or ex-Christians might ask just about the same questions as do Christians (thus illustrating, by the way, Wuthnow's point that we never entirely escape questions of the faith with which we are raised).

The problem is in what is meant by "distinct." Often when we say "Christian scholarship" people assume that we mean *uniquely* Christian scholarship. That impression is reinforced by the fact that some Christian scholars themselves speak of "distinctively Christian scholarship" as though they meant *uniquely* Christian scholarship. Often what they really have in mind is that Christian scholarship should reflect commitments to some distinct set of Christian teachings, including doctrines like the Trinity, the Incarnation, or Jesus' resurrection from the dead, as opposed to a general religious moralism. However, when it comes to applications to scholarship outside of theology itself, these distinctive Christian teachings seldom dictate scholarship that is distinctive in the sense that a non-Christian might not say more or less the same thing on a given topic.

These two senses of distinctiveness are easily confused. Distinctively Christian theological commitments do not usually lead to questions and agendas that other scholars might not share. Consider an analogy. One would hardly argue that because virtually any question or scholarly agenda that might be proposed by a Marxist scholar could be posed by a non-Marxist that therefore a distinctive Marxism was not shaping the scholarship. For Christianity the same applies.[11] Even on some questions of larger significance, distinctive Christian commitments do not necessarily produce agendas, questions, or conclusions that will not be almost identical to those of some other scholars. So Christians would do well to make clear that "distinctively Christian scholarship" does not typically lead to scholarship that will set Christians apart from everyone else.

This may be the place to emphasize that there is nothing inherently anti-Jewish in the call to reflect on the implications of Christianity for scholarship. Exactly the same general principles apply to practicing Jews or devotees of other faiths as should apply to various sorts of Christians. Those believers from the world religions that affirm the authority of the Hebrew Scriptures have reason to stand on virtually common ground on almost all the issues we have been discussing. In fact they may have far more in common intellectually with believers from kindred faiths than they will with those who have rejected the theistic tenets of their own religious heritage. Of course, standing on practically the same ground is no guarantee that believers of various faiths (or of the same faith) will agree. In any case, Jew and Christian rarely constitute the relevant divide with respect to the sorts of scholarly issues we are discussing. If questions of religiously based scholarship could be treated more as intellectual questions belonging to the quest for truth, rather than as political questions (which too often have plagued the relationships in the past), then scholars from these two faiths should increasingly see themselves as allies.

Another factor that constantly confuses the discussion of "Christian" scholarship is that there is no one Christian view on any subject, any more than there is one Jewish, Islamic, or Buddhist view. Serious Christians (to say nothing of nominal ones) differ so thoroughly on so many subjects, that it seems bizarre—particularly to outsiders—to talk about *the* Christian view of this or that. What people usually mean when they talk *the* Christian view is the view of a particular sub-tradition of Christianity. Even then there are countless disagreements and mutually contradictory assertions. What all the schools of Christian scholarship do have in common, however, is just the sort of thing that Robert Wuthnow describes as fundamental in the relationship of a tradition to scholarship—they are asking some common questions that have a direct relationship to their faith. Among these is the crucial underlying question: "How should our faith relate to our scholarship?" Despite the lack of Christian consensus in answering this question, it often leads scholars in particular traditions and communities to just the sorts of academic debates that can lead to new insights.

The point is, then, that the differences that Christian scholarship makes will show up in so many ways as to defy classification and easy formulae. Influences vary with the type of Christianity, the type of individual, the field and sub-field of scholarship, and the types of traditions of interpretation currently available. Given the bewildering varieties of permutations that can result from these and other factors, it is understandable that people object to speaking of any one approach or conclusion as "*the* Christian" view. At the same time, however, the diffuseness of Christian influences should not be mistaken for an absence of Christian influences. Those who are living the question of what is the relationship of their faith to their scholarship will answer it in countless ways.

CHALLENGING WHAT IS TAKEN FOR GRANTED

Historian Harry Stout has reflected perceptively on the subtle yet substantive influence of particular theological commitments. Speaking of his own work in American Puritan studies, Stout observed that one certainly does not have to be a Christian to take Puritans' beliefs seriously. In fact, two giants in the field who have done the most to rehabilitate respect for Puritan theology have been Perry Miller and his student, Edmund S. Morgan, both self-proclaimed atheists. Despite Stout's great admiration for these historians, he found his own work on Puritanism moving in some importantly different directions, reflecting his spiritual autobiography. First, the topic he chose was the history of the Puritan sermon. Despite the huge industry of American Puritan studies and vast manuscript resources of ordinary Sunday sermons, no previous scholar had bothered to delve deeply into these rich sources.

In addition, without much initial reflection on the theological roots of his interests, Stout found himself asking a different set of questions about these sermons and Puritan history than had been asked by previous scholars. Even historians so sympathetic to the Puritans as Miller and Morgan had been interested primarily in the origins of the American nation. Miller had talked about the New England "Mind" on the supposition that human ideas are essentially what history is. Stout, on the other hand, was more interested in the Puritan church than in the American nation, and he was interested more in "faith" than in "Mind" as a basic factor in human history. That meant that not only were Puritan theological debates of interest, but so were "other more interior themes of piety, spirituality, meditation, devotion, or conversion—all of which minimized conflicts and represented the stable bedrock on which an enduring Puritan religiosity was built."

Stout went further to observe that such sensibilities carried him beyond simply being open to a different set of categories or questions. It also eliminated certain interpretive agendas common to the profession. For example, this meant "that an event such as the Great Awakening was not explored simply for its social or political significance, but as a spiritual phenomenon that could not be wholly reduced to naturalistic categories." Anyone familiar with Stout's scholarship will recognize that he is not lacking in sensitivity to social, psychological, and political factors in history. In fact, his much acclaimed biography of George Whitefield, the leading revivalist of the Great Awakening, has been criticized by some more partisan Christian historians for not sufficiently emphasizing spiritual and providential themes. Stout holds to the contrary that while Christians should be open to spiritual influences they must not pretend to read the mind of God in assessing spiritual significance. Furthermore, he points out, although there is a long Christian tradition of hagiography, the even older biblical tradition of writing history depicts its heroes as deeply flawed. Despite this realism, Stout insists that openness to spiritual influences changes how Christians are likely to interpret Christian history itself. As he puts it:

> In particular we are warned against the sin of misplaced reductionism that would have us interpret the church and the community of faith—flawed and incomplete as it is—as epiphenomenal. Christian historians must eschew the secular tendency to treat religion simply as the outward manifestation of deeper, more fundamental realities that can be defined and understood solely in naturalistic terms.[12]

### CHALLENGING NATURALISTIC REDUCTIONISM

Stout's observations carry the discussion beyond differing scholarly agendas and questions, to another dimension of Christian scholarship—its function as a critique of current scholarly assumptions. Many scholars are oblivious to the first principles that they take for granted when they are initiated into contemporary scholarly communities. Despite the immense productivity of scholars examining everything else imaginable, relatively few of them look critically at the traditions of modern scholarship itself. Like Marxists, feminists, or postmodern deconstructionists, dissenters from the liberal mainstream, Christians have a place to stand that ought to lead them to reflect on which aspects of the current traditions fit well with their faith and which do not.

Although Christians have many reasons to appreciate and to support the rules and structures of liberal academia, they should be critical of what some have referred to as "the myth of liberal neutrality." As Lee Hardy, a philosopher at Calvin College, points out, liberal polity has a definite ideological bias. Hardy writes:

> The liberal project of tolerance was to construct a clean, open, and expansive public square based on rational consensus, while all weirdness and particularity is shuffled off and consigned to private chambers. In a liberal society people would be free to hold to any tradition-bound beliefs they like, as long as they agree not to act on them in public. But if the modernist presumption of common reason that underlies this method is itself a constituent of a particular tradition—

the western Enlightenment tradition—then the pretense to neutrality on the part of liberal tolerance begins to look more like a stratagem with a definite secular bias. The self-appointed referee turns out to be a contestant in disguise.[13]

Hardy's point that liberalism itself is an ideological tradition has been made by many religious philosophers, probably most effectively by the eminent Catholic thinker Alasdair MacIntyre, in *Three Rival Versions of Moral Enquiry* (1990).[14] Nicholas Wolterstorff, one of the leading philosophers in the Reformed tradition, adds that the liberal tradition of what constitutes "the good" is shaped by the demands of capitalism.[15] Liberal capitalism creates a public interest in suppressing the authority of all traditions except liberalism itself. For our purposes, as we have seen in earlier chapters, the most relevant part of the liberal tradition is that it prefers secular accounts of reality. One can well understand why things might seem to go more smoothly with such accounts, and some would argue that considerations of the public good ought to outweigh concerns of particular religious traditions. Others would argue, as Wolterstorff does, that the liberal tradition is unable to provide a coherent account of "the good" for a diverse society, as our public schools illustrate. Whatever one's position in such debates, however, it is naive to think of the liberal polity as being ideologically neutral.

The same point can be made with respect to many of the assumptions about scholarship that have emerged out of liberalism. As Stout's reflections illustrate, sometimes the differences in what is taken for granted result in subtle, but nonetheless substantial, differences in scholarship. In the field of history, for instance, the dominant liberal story has been some version of what shapes "the public good." Interest in that important subject has tended to preempt other themes such as those that would recognize room for spiritual concerns. American history writing, whether shaped by older emphases on consensus and politics or more recent attention to diversity and the common people, has been overwhelmingly dominated by secular accounts of what contributes to the public good. Even though in recent years there has been much capable work by historians of American religion, such work has seldom been incorporated into the mainstream historical canon. American history textbooks are notoriously deficient on this score, especially when they deal with anything after 1740. Many of the "best" history departments do not even offer courses on religious history, nor is it often dealt with in other courses. It is not that the leading historians who control such things think that religion is historically unimportant. If you asked them, most would say that it is important. Nonetheless, they have been so shaped by a culture which accounts for "the good" without reference to religion that they do not notice religion's absence.[16]

In an earlier chapter we looked at how one of the most pervasive assumptions of modern scholarship—scientific naturalism—gained its sway. Scientific naturalism is, of course, a very useful methodological stance, which Christians employ all the time in the technical aspects of their scholarship. However, like the liberal culture of which it is a part, scientific naturalism is not ideologically neutral. Sometimes the bias of scientific naturalism against religious and spiritual concerns is made explicit, as by those natural scientists who use it as the basis for a metaphysical worldview. They proclaim that knowledge gained by empirical observation is the only knowledge there is. This is the view presented, for instance, by Carl Sagan in his famous television series *Cosmos.* He begins in almost biblical cadence, "The Cosmos is all that is or ever was or ever will be."[17] What he means is that there is no reality beyond the physical universe. What Sagan fails to mention is that this viewpoint is not itself based on scientific evidence, but rather is a premise of modern thought.

Most scholars are not as blunt as Sagan and may not even believe that physical reality is all there is, but their scholarship is built around a tradition that operates as though that were the case. As Stout's observations suggest, the difference for Christians has not so much to do with what other scholars include—such as social, economic, or political factors—as with what they exclude. Furthermore, the distinguishing feature of Christian scholars working in mainstream academic settings is not that they are going to identify the workings of the Holy Spirit in the Great Awakening or use God to explain any gaps in current scientific theory, but rather they do not believe that empirically demonstrable explanations are the only, or even the most important, explanations. This openness sets their other calculations and theories in a different context and hence subtly changes their implications and relative importance. No matter how wonderful our scientific explanations of the working of the cosmos, we should not stumble into the unfounded conclusion that the physical cosmos is all there is. No matter how ingenious our explanation of how George Whitefield sparked the Great Awakening, we will not likely tell the story as though that exhausts the explanation.

The larger issue is reductionism. Once we have a convincing explanation at the level of empirically researched connections we are inclined to think we have a complete explanation. The late Donald M. MacKay, a specialist in brain physiology, has provided some helpful reflections on this problem from the perspective of one who is both a scientist and a Christian. The physiological story of how the brain operates is vastly different from the subjective experience of its operation. Each account is in a sense true and complete at its own level. In another sense, however, it would distort our account if we insisted that only the level that we are working from provides the true story. In particular, the microscopic story that the brain physiologist can tell would be wildly misleading if it denied significance to the subject's own account of her thoughts.

MacKay suggests as an analogy the various interpretations to which an electronic advertising sign, such as one might see on Broadway, might be subject. An electrician may be able to give a very accurate and thorough account of the electrical operation of the sign. We would not fault the electrician for failing to mention what the sign said—that is not part of his technical analysis. We would fault him, however, if he acted as though his was the only important meaning of the sign. To elaborate on MacKay's image, let's say the sign says "LIVE GIRLS." Once we know that, the sign takes on significance at many other levels. We can imagine a group of sociologists discussing the social significance of the sign. Or next we see a group of economists debating its marketing significance. Experts on gender would see it as essentially about sexual exploitation. Politicians might worry about controversies it would generate. Ethicists would debate its morality. Linguists might discuss the ambiguity of the syntax. Aestheticians might debate whether it is kitsch or simply tasteless. And so forth. Each of these accounts may be complete at its own level, but if it denies the significance of the others it is incomplete and misleading. To describe the tendency of specialists to reduce their interpretations to "nothing but" what they can account for in their own disciplines MacKay uses the somewhat greasy, but memorable, label, "nothing buttery."[18]

As a scientist, MacKay emphasized the complementary character of modes of knowing—that each is in a sense complete at its own level as long as practitioners acknowledge the validity of other levels. That model works better in strictly technical disciplines than it does in our example of the electronic sign which can be analyzed in terms of many disciplines other than merely technical. Even though the economists may want to talk only about the economic significance of the sign, they should be listening to what the sociologists, political scientists, and others are saying about it. It is not even strictly true that the work of the electrician will be unaffected by the larger meaning. One can well imagine some of the gender experts and ethicists insisting that the electrician should refuse work on the sign because of its LIVE GIRLS message. Certainly if the sign said DOWN WITH JEWISH POWER most people would want the technicians to refuse work. So the principle is not that larger meaning never should alter technical work. Sometimes it will and should.

In the mid-nineteenth century, at the outset of the era of modern specialization, John Henry Newman provided one of the most insightful Christian critiques of academic reductionism. In his famous lectures, published as *The Idea of the University,* speaking as the founding rector of the Catholic University of Ireland, Newman reflected on how the modern disciplines were ignoring the relevance of theological perspectives. Newman argued that since a university's purpose was to deal with all knowledge, and since theology was surely a branch of knowledge, the university ought to have a place for theology. By this he did not mean simply that a university should include a theology department. Rather, he was arguing from the premise that all knowledge is connected. Truths from one realm of knowledge ultimately need to be qualified by those from other realms. "A true enlargement of the mind," he writes, ". . . is the power of viewing many things at once as one whole, of referring them severally to their true place in the universal system, of understanding their respective values, and determining their mutual dependence." Hence, for those who believe God is at the heart of reality, other knowledge is distorted if divorced from the context of theological truths.

The problem with the university as it was emerging, said Newman, was that each branch of knowledge tended to aggrandize its own perspective.[19] We can see the results much more strikingly today, although we tend to take them for granted. Practitioners of each academic specialty tend to talk only to members of their own discipline or sub-discipline and only in their own specialized language and categories. Psychologists may reduce all belief to responses to early psychic needs. Biologists may see only a struggle for genes to survive. Anthropologists may interpret all human history in terms of evolutionary survival mechanisms. And so forth.

Even when reductionism is not so extreme, modern academia leans heavily toward what might be called naturalistic reductionism. Even when the big picture is taken into account, it is a picture that includes everything but God. So even if we do not have "nothing buttery," we are still left with "everything buttery."

It is easy to understand why competing theologies were excluded when trying to build a cooperative yet pluralistic academia. But that is another question. Now we are talking about whether that exclusion makes any difference in day-to-day academia. Surely the big picture would change for academics who believe that God is at the center of that picture. And many of their other academic insights would be affected if they developed the habit of asking how they fit into that big picture.

The problem of recognizing the day-to-day significance of this factor is aggravated by the difficulty of talking about something that is missing. Not only is it missing, but its absence is taken for granted. Recently I talked to a television reporter who was working on a story on religion in higher education but having trouble convincing her producer and anchorman that there was any story. How do you portray something that is missing? Students who are attuned to theological perspectives can tell when professors are analyzing things in ways that exclude spiritual dimensions or diminish religious outlooks. Often, however, like the dog that did not bark, the differences are not noticed.

CHALLENGING THE TRANSCENDENT SELF

The scientific naturalism of the past century has typically been accompanied by lavish celebrations of humanity. A characteristic example of the subtle challenges to traditional faiths that are likely to be encountered in university classrooms can be seen in the recent PBS television series *The Human Quest,* a popular summation of some current academic trends. This series brings together in philosophically sophisticated ways some of the latest thinking from a variety of academic fields to tell the story of the ongoing human quest for successful evolutionary adaptation. Despite many helpful insights, ultimately the story that it tells is that of the triumph of the scientific imagination. At the same time, however, the series assures viewers this scientific outlook is not opposed to spiritual values or even the search for God. The commentary points out that Einstein, after all, believed in a God who produced orderly laws of nature. "Science is not an assault on the human spirit," it assures over a musical background including "Hallelujah" chorales, "but an expression of the human spirit."

This assurance that the spiritual or even what we call "God" is not excluded by science masks the underlying message that traditional religions are passé. As one Christian commentator puts it, "*The Human Quest* seems to rest on the slightly veiled assumption that religious traditions are among those human adaptations that, according to science, the evolutionary process has selected against." That message is not presented in any overtly offensive way; yet for that reason it may be all the more effective.[20]

One of the most common outlooks in contemporary academia is something like that underlying *The Human Quest*. Strictly speaking this common point of view is not anti-religious. It may grant room for the spiritual or for "God," but these are treated as human creations, ultimately explained in naturalistic terms. From a traditional religious perspective, such an outlook might be seen as an alternative theology—one in which humans are at the center. Even if a particular version of this theology does not include any reference to "God," it is at least religious in celebrating transcendent values—although purely human ones. Reflecting ideals that have been current since the rise of nineteenth-century Romanticism, the human spirit is supreme in this view. Science itself is an expression of those higher human values that we find within. This can be an inspiring and productive ideal. As far as the question "What difference does it make?" is concerned, however, it should be apparent that this prevailing academic big picture is much different from that of traditional theologies.

Christian scholars, at least those with more traditional theological perspectives, should be critical of this absolutization of humanity. Christians, of course, have long emphasized human significance and the value even of those humans who may seem least significant. Yet such affirmations have been made in the context of recognizing human limits. As Pascal put it, humans' greatness lies in knowing we are wretched. Whatever the particulars of their views of human nature, Christians have traditionally been united in proclaiming that the heart of human sinfulness is the illusion that we can be our own gods, a law unto ourselves, creating and controlling our own reality.

This view of humanity, which originates in the Hebrew Scriptures, ought to transform religiously committed scholars into dissenters from many theories taken for granted in academia today. It should make them critical of viewpoints, especially prevalent in the arts and literature, that emphasize human freedom and creativity as supreme values. Although of immense worth, these human gifts will reach their highest expression when exercised within a sense of the limits of the individual in relationship to the community, the created order, and ultimately to God. Individuals who act as though they were a law unto themselves or who proclaim there is no law are apt to destroy those around them. Granted, excessive religious zeal is a danger as well. That does not change the fact that current philosophies which absolutize the self pose a real danger of fostering lawlessness.

Such philosophies pay their dividends in popular and celebrity culture, another area ripe for critique by scholars who see more to life than the self. Here again, as on MTV, creativity knows no limits, but not because the artistic goals are so high. Cynicism has become a cliché. Similarly the world of advertising and mass culture has no shame in exploiting the ideals of unlimited freedom in a way that cashes out as sensuality and self-indulgence. Scholars from all sorts of traditions might critique such cultural trends, but scholars with a theological perspective are more likely to see them as part of a larger pattern of almost cultic self-worship.

A number of Christian scholars have dwelt on such themes as they riddle our cultural life. Quentin Schultze and his colleagues examine this motif and others in popular culture in *Dancing in the Dark: Youth, Popular Culture, and the Electronic Media.*[21] In *Psychology as Religion: The Cult of Self-Worship,* Paul Vitz presents a sharp critique of this pervasive theme in his field. Perhaps the best-known critique, which although not presented explicitly as Christian scholarship certainly includes Christian themes, is that of Robert Bellah and his colleagues, *Habits of the Heart: Individualism and Commitment in American Life.*[22] Charles Taylor in his influential *Sources of the Self: The Making of Modern Identity* traces the rise of modern ideas of the self, growing out of Christian sources but then taking on a life of their own as a major myth of modernity and postmodernity.[23] The work of

Roger Lundin, discussed in the next chapter, emphasizes similar themes in literature. These and other comparable works illustrate how a variety of Christian perspectives, some more and some less explicit or developed, provide rich resources for cultural critiques.

## MORAL JUDGMENTS

So far we have managed to spell out the differences that a Christian perspective might make without developing a point that some assume is the whole of the discussion—that it will help shape moral judgments. Scholars, like all people, are moralists. Nothing is more common, as least in scholarship having to do with human behavior, than moral judgments, whether explicit or, more often, implicit. Moral judgments, like other commitments, help determine what subjects people study, what questions they ask about their subjects, and what answers they will give to those questions. This point seems so obvious that it is puzzling that scholars should raise questions, such as those cited at the opening of this chapter, about the relevance of faith to scholarship.

Probably the main reason why seemingly evident moral influences are missed is that people fall into the trap of confusing influence with uniqueness. Christians, they point out, have no monopoly on moral judgments. Furthermore, any moral evaluation that a Christian might make might just as well be made by a non-Christian.

One can appreciate why the point that Christianity makes a difference in moral judgments eludes some people of good will. Often, perhaps more often than not, Christians' moral values look remarkably like other currently prevalent sets of values. The agenda of one group of Christian academics will look much like the Democratic Party platform. That of another group will be conservative Republican. Liberationist Christians often sound like Marxists. And so forth. Christianity does not seem to be the variable.

One reason for such overlapping of moral judgments is that Christianity has played such a large role in shaping the moral principles that have become standard parts of the Western cultural heritage. Christian morality, usually wed to other traditions, has often taken on a life of its own without reference to its original theological parentage. So one of the great ironies in Western cultural history of the past two centuries is that many of the most effective attacks on traditional Christianity have taken place in the name of what amounts to a secularized Christian morality. Since at least the Enlightenment, critics of Christianity often have claimed the high ground of morality, presenting themselves as more humane, more just, more compassionate, more inclusive, and as the true champions of liberty and equality, of fraternity and sorority. All too often there has been some justice in these claims, especially those directed at Christian establishments. As a result, the lines between Christian and non-Christian morality are further blurred. Non-Christians often draw on the spirit of Christian morality to launch effective attacks on the forms of Christianity that provide sub-Christian rationales for established power.

Such attacks have been effective because in practice the morality of professing Christians has so often been compromised by too great a dependence on political, social, and economic establishments. Throughout history one can find debacles resulting from the identification of political causes with the cause of Christ. Those who cite the Crusades, the Inquisition, or Cromwell's excesses as arguments against Christianity are pointing to instances in which the faith has been coopted and corrupted by temptations to power.

This irony, that those who reject traditional theologies sometimes seem to follow principles consistent with Christian morality while Christians often do not, contributes to the confusion over the moral influences of Christianity on scholarship. In each case people are being shaped by the multiple cultural traditions of morality with which we are surrounded. Christian moral influences do not come to us unmixed with other concerns, interests, and beliefs. In our highly politicized age, we are particularly likely to have our moral agendas set by public opinion, which itself reflects a multiplicity of traditions of moral discourse. Self-interests further complicate the picture.

Yet all these ambiguities do not add up to an argument that Christian commitments either do not or should not make a difference in the moral agendas that so shape our scholarship. What the ambiguities suggest is that Christian commitments frequently do not make the sort of difference that they can and should. Often part of the problem is the very kind of thing we have been talking about, that Christians have often been too slow to challenge the conventional wisdom of their age. The past failure of

Christians consistently to follow the moral principles of their faith is a reason for them to cultivate more critical Christian thinking, not abandon it. If during the past century many of the best academic minds had been wrestling with the implications of their faith for scholarship, rather than shying away from the subject, perhaps we would have less unthinking appropriation of whatever moral conventions are currently in vogue.

Moral judgments are not the whole of Christian influence on scholarship. Rather they are part of a larger pattern of values that will set a scholar's academic agenda. Christian commitments make a difference to scholarship because scholars are whole people and the various aspects of their belief systems are interrelated. As the example of the gestalt images suggests, many particular aspects of a Christian scholar's work will look much like the work of a colleague with another nontheistic set of commitments. Yet the relative importance that we assign to things, the central questions we ask about them, and the assumptions that lie behind these questions will all vary according to what makes up our larger picture of reality. The differences in the larger picture for the religious person are ultimately theological differences. They are beliefs about God and how God relates to us and the rest of reality. So to get to specific examples of the positive contributions of Christianity to scholarship we must explore the ways in which a context of theological beliefs changes the way we value other things.

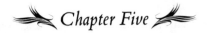

# Chapter Five

# The Positive Contributions
# of Theological Context

Scholars do not operate in a vacuum, but rather within the frameworks of their communities, traditions, commitments, and beliefs. Their scholarship, even when specialized, develops within a larger picture of reality. So we must ask: What is in that larger picture? Is there a place for God? If so, does God's presence make any difference to the rest of the picture? Does that presence change the relative proportions of the picture as a whole? A picture of reality in which there is a being great enough to produce and to oversee the universe is, after all, quite different from one in which things operate sheerly through impersonal forces. If we affirm a reality that includes a being of immense intelligence, power, and concern for us, every other fact or belief will have some relationship to that being. At the least the presence of that being should alter our view of the relative significance of the other aspects of reality that we deal with in our scholarship.

While God and theology should be considered as factors in our scholarship, we do not want to reduce our subjects to just their theological dimensions. (By theology here I do not mean primarily the discipline of theology, but rather any serious thought about God and God's revelation according to a particular religious tradition.) Such theological principles, important as they are, are just one point of reference that we should take into account in thinking about the significance of our work. So Christians can do the bulk of their academic work according to the standards and perspectives of their discipline, just as long as they are willing to keep in mind the context of theological concerns and be open to reflecting on their implications for larger questions.[1] When addressing the diverse academy most such reflection will exert its influence as background beliefs, although it is fair for Christian scholars to say conditionally: "Suppose someone believed in God, how would the assumptions or conclusions of our discipline look different?"

Because there are many Christian theologies and many academic disciplines, it is impossible to present a simple set of rules for how theology might be integrated with other scholarship. What we can do, however, is consider a few examples based on some the most common Christian points of doctrine.

## CREATION

Most of the examples offered so far have to do with the affirmation that God is the creator of heaven and earth. This claim of Christianity and kindred religions has momentous scholarly implications. In fact, one way to describe the history of modern Western thought is as a rejection of the doctrine of creation and its systematic exclusion as a consideration in academic study, outside of theology itself. Even scholars who do believe in creation are expected to act, as Peter Berger has put it, on the basis of "methodological atheism."[2]

Many people think of this as applying primarily to the natural sciences, where it does indeed have bearing on larger speculations, but it actually has far more pervasive implications in the humanities and the social sciences. Methodological atheism in these fields means that humans and their cultures have to be regarded as nothing more than the products of natural processes. With God eliminated a priori, there is no other approach that makes sense.

If Christian scholars who believe in creation begin to question this arbitrary dogma that scholars must view humans as no more than products of purely natural forces, it will have far-reaching implications in the humanities, the social sciences, and in the study of religion itself. Much of the difference will appear in critiques of prevailing naturalistic first principles. An impressive example of such Christian scholarship is John Milbank's *Theology and Social Theory: Beyond Secular Reason,* a work that challenges the fundamental assumptions of the social sciences and much of religious studies.[3]

Such a challenge to first principles would have important implications for questions of morality. If considerations about God are a priori eliminated from consideration, then the most satisfactory contemporary accounts of human morality seem to many scholars to be those that posit that moral standards evolved as survival mechanisms and to serve various cultural interests. Some philosophers do, of course, propose ways to avoid the moral relativism that this starting point may lead to, and many people find these alternative moralities persuasive.[4] Many other people think that the premise of an indifferent universe points most naturally to the conclusion that no moral standards are absolute. One common corollary is that moral standards are to be valued only insofar as a person or a group approves of the cultural functions they perform. According to this widely held view, all we are left with are our interests, our group loyalties, and our preferences.

Christian scholars' work may also involve analysis of how humans construct moral systems to serve cultural functions, but that analysis will take place in an entirely different framework. Ultimately, they will insist, principles of morality originate with God. God has provided humans with a moral law which, however imperfectly we may understand it, should be our guide.[5] All cultural constructions of morality are thus not in principle equal. Some are closer to what God approves and some are further away. One may need to be modest in making judgments on many fine points. On the other hand, Christians should see themselves as working within a universe of God-created laws in which some acts are simply wrong, while others come closer to divine standards. For instance, Christians believe that the principle of altruism—that the weak should be cared for by the strong—is not just a cultural construct but a norm given by God to all of humanity.

As we have seen, Christians often disagree among themselves about the moral implications of the Christian faith. One group of Christians may insist that Christians may in no circumstances participate in warfare and that they must do all they can to seek disarmament. Others may be equally insistent that in some circumstances warfare is justified and that unqualified Christian pacifism would be the surest way to invite warfare. Nevertheless, these two groups would be in agreement that Christians should be peacemakers, even though they might disagree deeply regarding how that is best accomplished. Both groups of Christians in this debate, furthermore, would agree that there are normative standards of God's will that they should seek to follow and that Christ's command to be peacemakers is an important reason to work for peace. Even in cases in which Christians flatly disagree on what is the proper moral principle, they at least agree that there are principles higher than their own preferences or those of their group.

Whatever Christians' particular applications of their moral principles, such questions provide an important opening for dialogue with those in the pluralistic academy. Most of those who deny the relevance of theism to academic inquiry nonetheless hold very strong opinions about what is right and wrong. They may strongly advocate, for instance, equal treatment for women and minorities. Yet given the naturalism to which they have limited themselves, it is difficult to see how they have an adequate basis for their seemingly absolutist moral claims.

Recently *The Chronicle of Higher Education* carried an essay by an anthropologist, Carolyn Fluehr-Lobban, agonizing over the failure of practitioners of her discipline to face up to their moral responsibilities. Anthropology, she pointed out, has long been dominated by the dogma of cultural relativism. Yet how ought Western scholars to reconcile that dogma with practices of other cultures that they find deeply offensive, such as female genital mutilation, violence toward women generally, or racial genocide? On the one hand, Fluehr-Lobban recognized the force of the standard contemporary academician's question, "What authority do we Westerners have to impose our own concept of universal rights on the rest of humanity?" To that question she had no good theoretical answer. On the other hand, her deep aversion to the practices and her loyalty to a feminist community concerned for women's welfare forced her to conclude that "when there is a choice between defending human rights and defending cultural relativism, anthropologists should choose to promote human rights."[6]

Fluehr-Lobban's dilemma is symptomatic of the state of higher education today, even when it may be at its best. The problem is not, as is often alleged, a lack of moral concern. Many academics have deep moral and political convictions. What they most typically lack is the ability to provide a compelling intellectual rationale for these beliefs consistent with their other intellectual commitments. For at least the past two generations cultural relativism of one sort or another has been essential for dismantling various Western traditions that many progressive-minded academics find oppressive. There seems to be no consistent way, however, to keep such principles from dissolving the moral traditions they themselves affirm.

The moral impasse arrived at by some of the most progressive of contemporary academics is well illustrated in a symposium on "Freedom and Interpretation" sponsored by Amnesty International. The participants were to consider the implications of "the deconstruction of the self for the liberal tradition." Specifically they were asked: "Does the self as construed by the liberal tradition still exist? If not, whose human rights are we defending?" The challenge they faced was the proposition, as Tzvetan Todorov put it, "that it is not possible, without inconsistency, to defend human rights with one hand and deconstruct the idea of humanity on the other." The participants in the symposium took up this challenge, proposing various ingenious ways to reconstruct principles of universal rights after the old liberal tradition of individual rights has been discarded. One participant, Wayne C. Booth, offered a particularly revealing observation:

> It is true that some postmodernist theorists of the social self have not explicitly acknowledged the religious implications of what they are about. But if you read them closely, you will see that more and more of them are talking about the human mystery in terms that resemble those of the subtlest traditional theologians.

Even though postmodern theorists reject traditional views of God, they may well end up investing humans with qualities just as mysterious.[7]

In a purely naturalistic universe postmodern criticisms of the old liberal effort to invest *Homo sapiens* with "human rights" may make sense; yet it is difficult to see what can replace it that will not be vulnerable to the same criticisms. If one believes that our species is no more than what has so far evolved, there is hardly a convincing basis for treating all people as having equal rights or for special concerns for the weak and the disadvantaged.[8] Christian theism, on the other hand, at least provides grounds for supporting the moral intuitions that many academics share. Without theism, in a world where all moral systems are seen as simply constructions of interested groups, many people find it difficult (despite the many efforts at justification) to defend the moral claims of one group over those of another. Ultimately, as Nietzsche long ago recognized and many postmoderns have reaffirmed, the only effective arbiter of contested moral claims is power—or perhaps in our culture we should add hype. According to Christianity, on the other hand, we should love our neighbors and even our enemies, since we are all creatures of the same loving Creator. Lacking such a principle, it becomes a Herculean task for contemporary academics to defend with logical consistency such common beliefs as that all humans should be treated as sisters or brothers.

This is not to say that Christianity does not have its own intellectual problems, mysteries, and moral dilemmas. Certainly it does (even if Christians may see these problems as less troubling than the alternatives). For the moment, however, the issue is not whether Christianity is intellectually, morally, and spiritually more satisfying than other options. Rather, the point is that if one puts the doctrine of a creator into the picture it will substantially change how one thinks about such issues as human rights and moral principles.

The doctrine of creation also has important implications in the field of epistemology. Questions of "how we know" are fundamental to all disciplines. Here traditional Christians have reason to agree with the postmodern relativists; modern scholars are up a creek without an epistemic paddle. That is just where biblical and Christian tradition says pure naturalism will lead. Human perceptions are notoriously limited and, with God excluded from consideration, it is difficult to find a point of reference for establishing any certainty in what we claim to know. Christian scholars, on the other hand, begin with God's creation as an organizing premise for understanding what they observe. If we start with faith in the creator God as one of our first principles, then modern epistemic problems are cast in a new light. For one thing, if God has created our minds as well as the rest of reality, then it makes sense to believe that God may communicate with us in nature as well as in Scripture, even if as "through a glass darkly." In such a theistic framework, we have reason to suppose that God would have created us with some mechanisms for distinguishing truth from error, however darkened our hearts and puny our intellects. Many questions remain in this area and again Christians disagree strongly among themselves.[9] Particularly important are intra-Christian debates as to how far the optimistic implications of belief in theistic creation are offset by the Christian doctrine of the fall of humans into sin. At the least we can say that with God in the picture the set of epistemological questions changes dramatically.

Taking seriously the doctrine of creation gives Christians a critical place to stand in recent debates about postmodern epistemologies. Having discovered the defects of Enlightenment epistemic optimism and objectivism, postmodernism has lurched to the relativist or even nihilist extreme of insisting that all our "reality" is an ad hoc social construction. But as Diogenes Allen points out, despite its radicalism, postmodernism retains the two central pillars of the modern mentality: "belief in a self-contained universe, and belief in unlimited human freedom."[10] Within the framework of these two givens, postmodern relativism seems to some to rise to the top as the best explanatory theory. If, on the other hand, a Christian believes both that God created reality and that human reason is limited, other alternatives open up. For instance, the Christian framework can provide a good account for our actual experience of encountering a real world, in ways limited by our commitments, social positions, and prejudices.

Roger Lundin in *The Culture of Interpretation: Christian Faith and the Postmodern World* provides some excellent examples of how contemporary debates in literary theory look different when Christian theological perspectives are allowed into the picture. In Lundin's view most of the discussion of art and literature during the past two centuries has been controlled by the absolutization of the human self. With the traditional Christian Creator effectively barred from cutting-edge theory, the human creator assumed mammoth proportions. At first, in the romantic movement, this exaltation of the self was supposed to bring out greater access to the transcendent, as in Ralph Waldo Emerson's apotheosis of the artist. Even after the demise of idealistic philosophies to support such outlooks, romantic conceptions of the self, particularly of the self as creator, persisted. So throughout the twentieth century the manifestation of one's own creative vision has been used to justify almost any artistic expression. With the postmodern denial that we can have any access to a transcendent or to any metanarrative except its own (that humans are the only creators) some of the modern aura of the artist as redeemer was transferred to the critic as redeemer. The critic with the power to historicize and relativize every text (and all of life could be seen as a "text") became a person freed from convention because he recognized that everything was convention.

Ultimately, argues Lundin, the question is one of authority. Traditionally in Christianity God was thought of as the *author* of the universe and of history. In the modern West, however, the elite champions of high culture have urged throwing off any authority external to human beings themselves. Lundin cites W. H. Auden's poem, *The Sea and the Mirror,* which in its opening section asks, "O what authority gives / Existence its surprise?" Human beings, according to Auden, having rejected external authority, inevitably make either the minds or the body their supreme lord. Only when, as Auden puts it, we "see ourselves as we are, neither cosy nor playful, but swaying out on the ultimate wind-whipped cornice that overhangs the unabiding void" will we be able to hear "the real Word that is our only *raison d'être.* . . . [I]t is just here, among the ruins and the bones, that we may rejoice in the perfected Work which is not our own."[11]


## THE INCARNATION


The doctrine of divine creation has the widest implications for scholarship in Christian and other monotheistic traditions, but Christians should ask as well whether more specifically Christian theological beliefs might also have implications for their scholarship. The Christian faith that Jesus Christ is God, the second person of the Trinity, who was incarnated as truly human, is central to Christian tradition. If such an astonishing belief is deeply imbedded in the web of beliefs that forms our thoughts, what implications ought it to have for our academic work?

One implication, which is not unique to Christianity but is accentuated by faith in Christ as God incarnate, is that the supernatural and the natural realms are not closed off to each other. Christians who affirm that Jesus was not only human but also fully divine must presuppose that the transcendent God, the wholly Other, the Creator of heaven and earth, can appear and be known in our ordinary history. Most of modern thought, by contrast, assumes something like "Lessing's ditch": that one cannot get from the contingent truths of history to the timeless metaphysical truths of religion. Acceptance of the incarnation, however, seems to presuppose that we *can* know about the transcendent through ordinary contingent means, such as the testimony of others and evidence drawn from our own experience. The Christian experience of faith involves in some way knowing God through an encounter with the historical person, Jesus Christ. The starting point for Christian thought, then, entails an implicit rejection of the rule (perhaps derived from more abstract conceptions of the deity in classical Greek thought) that we cannot bridge the gap between empirical truths and wider metaphysical realities. Religious truths are not first of all "necessary truths," like the truths of mathematics, but rather, according to Christianity, revealed to us in encounters with the divine person within our history.

Christians who believe in the incarnation are then working within a framework of a universe that is open to spiritual phenomena that go beyond what people of all faiths or of no formal faith can agree on. Christians may be as skeptical as anyone about any particular claim of a miracle, a revelation, or spiritual phenomenon, but they would not rule it out on the modern premise that such things do not happen. In short, they are working in a spiritually open, rather than closed, universe.

At the same time, in academic and many other settings, Christians may engage in what could be called "methodological secularization." For a particular task, such as landing an airplane, this is the stance that we hope our fellow citizens will take. No matter how open the pilot may be to spiritual realities, we hope that he will rely on the radar and not just the Holy Spirit when trying to get to O'Hare. The same applies in many academic activities, especially the more technical ones. Yet the implication of such methodological secularization is different from that of the "methodological atheism" which is more often the academic rule.[12] Methodological secularization means only that for limited ad hoc purposes we will focus on natural phenomena accessible to all, while not denying their spiritual dimensions as created and ordered by God or forgetting that there is much more to the picture. The pilot who follows the radar and the instrument panel may even sense those tasks differently if she believes she is ultimately dependent on God and that she has spiritual responsibility to her passengers. As we have said repeatedly, in academic work such openness may have real impact on our theories, particularly in eliminating those which claim that the universally accessible natural phenomena are all there is.

For Christians in the natural sciences, this incarnationally based viewpoint should invite a consciousness of the wider context of the more real and more permanent spiritual dimensions of reality within which empirical inquiry takes place. This awareness might have an impact on how one regards the significance of one's work, even if, technically considered, that work might look much like the work of a nontheist. When scientists have

occasion to articulate their understanding of the wider context—philosophical, historical, or practical—for what they do, this wider consciousness may have explicit implications as well. Since Christ the Word is
co-creator of all existence according to Christian doctrine, scientists with
strongly incarnational views of nature may be sensitive to spiritual dimensions in all of reality. Practically speaking such views might affect how one
applies scientific or technological inquiry to issues such as ecology, medi-
cine, or engineering.[13] For some pure researchers, simply the doxological
implications of an incarnational worldview may be sufficient. They might
resonate with the sensibilities of Gerard Manley Hopkins:

> The world is charged with the grandeur of God.
>   It will flame out, like shining from shook foil;
>   It gathers to a greatness, like the ooze of oil
> Crushed. . . .[14]

Such sensibilities might not change one's research methods or conclusions. Nevertheless, they might have an impact both on the quality of one's
work and on one's agenda in studying God's creation in the first place.
Surely there would be huge implications when such scientists relate their
subjects to the larger issues of life. At the least it would counter the impression, created by some scientific popularizers, that because natural science is
essentially materialistic, materialism therefore provides the best account of
reality.

The incarnational motif also has implications for the arts, humanities,
and social sciences. It suggests, for instance, that we may see God working
in the ordinary, if only we have the eyes to see. Poets, artists, and musicians
may be most open to giving expression to such dimensions of reality, but
they are there for all to perceive.

For the Christian the incarnation is not an abstraction; it is central to
the revelation of the character of God. As Jonathan Edwards emphasizes,
God is not only a righteous judge, but is also infinitely loving. God is not
only revealing the beauty of his love in creation, but displays the highest
love and hence the highest beauty in Christ's dying for us, the infinitely
good God incarnate dying on behalf of those who despise him. Although
we are creatures capable of great love, we in fact build our universes

around love to our selves. God's display of his sacrificial love to us in Christ relativizes our self-righteousness. United with Christ, we are to love even those whom we would naturally despise.

This revelation of the character of God in Christ should thus change our sensibilities toward other humans. In the incarnation, Christ emptied himself and became poor for our sake. He identified with the poor and the ordinary. Christ went so far as to instruct us that when we see the poor and the destitute we see him. How we act toward them is an indicator of how we love him. Christ's incarnation honors what the world has not usually honored.

Once again we run into a central irony in attempting to isolate the implications of Christian commitments for our scholarship. The sensibilities of Christians toward the poor and the weak have been dulled by the very success of the assimilation of these same sensibilities by the wider Western culture and lately world culture. Sometime in the last four centuries many Westerners began attacking hierarchies and emphasizing the essential equality of all humans. Often such ideas had direct religious roots, as in early Quakerism or in the pietism and other forms of "religion of the heart" of the seventeenth and eighteenth centuries. In other instances, the religious roots, although substantial, might be less apparent. Some prevalent modern political sentiments grew out of the covenantal idea that divine law stood above rulers as well as ruled, and evolved into talk of "the rights of men" and eventually "the rights of women." At least by the time of the French Revolution, the flowerings of such sensibilities were often separated from their Christian roots. In fact whatever spirit of Christianity they embodied was often being opposed by institutional Christianity. So, while in the nineteenth and twentieth centuries many Christian expressions of such sensibilities have persisted, they have been overshadowed by their non-Christian or anti-Christian counterparts. Marxism's concern for the poor is the most obvious example. Eventually the rootlessness of such humanitarianism caught up with Marxism. One of the great tasks of Christian scholarship is to recover some dimensions of Christian teaching which have been alienated from their theological roots. This task is particularly urgent in an era when secular morality is adrift and traditional Christianity itself is too often beholden to the politics of self-interest and simplistic solutions.

## THE HOLY SPIRIT AND THE SPIRITUAL
## DIMENSIONS OF REALITY

The influences on scholarship of Christian beliefs in God's creation and incarnation are not entirely separable from the implications of faith in the continuing work of the Holy Spirit. Such interrelatedness is, of course, just what one would expect from a Trinitarian faith. Both the creation and the incarnation presuppose that we must be open to the spiritual dimension of things, and belief in the Holy Spirit should underscore that point.

The Christian doctrine of the Holy Spirit involves not only the affirmation that God's Spirit is actively working in history but also that the Holy Spirit works in our own lives. Jonathan Edwards describes Christians' spiritual sensibilities as like a sixth sense. The Bible, he points out, frequently depicts Christians' experience as like being given eyes to see or ears to hear. Our hearts in their natural state are ultimately closed off by self-love. Even our most elaborate projects for doing good suffer from this limitation. Ultimately, all that we do without God is drawn back into the black hole of our selfishness (to use a contemporary image that Edwards would have relished). In regeneration, however, the Holy Spirit enters into our hearts so that we can get a glimpse of the overwhelming love and beauty of God, epitomized in Christ's suffering and death for such unworthy creatures as ourselves. When we have eyes to see this love and beauty we are drawn to it and, in principle at least, away from our selfishness. With our hearts opened even slightly to the indwelling of the Holy Spirit, or infinite love of God, our center of gravity is changed. Rather than being preoccupied with self-love we begin to have a love for all being, or all that promotes good. With spiritual eyes we can see God speaking in the beauties of nature and in the beauties of Christ manifested in our neighbors.

This is not to assert a Christian gnosticism, as some might accuse. As should be clear by now, we are not talking about bringing a secret Christian knowledge into our scholarship but rather about cultivating sensibilities. Christians of course do believe some different things about reality than do non-Christians, and these beliefs can reshape other important relationships. But the particulars of Christian belief are open to anyone as far as they are propositions about reality. When we talk of a sixth spiritual sense, however, we are talking about what Christians consider to be the grace to keep in mind (or to have the heart for) a sense of higher reality and its implications, even as we deal with the mundane in otherwise pedestrian ways. For scholarship the primary practical result of such a sense is to sustain the motive to wrestle with the questions of the relationships between the two dimensions of reality which shape our experience.

Christian scholarship should be marked by a healthy sense of the limits of human knowledge. One of the fundamental characteristics of a spiritual sensibility is the recognition that there are immense dimensions of reality of which we have only the dimmest awareness. The very nature of spiritual reality is mysterious, so that we have only the most general notions of its meanings. One of the most common mistakes of Christian thinkers has been to fail to recognize the limits of their own knowledge of the mysterious spiritual realm. For instance, Christians have often confused the belief *that* the Holy Spirit is working in history and in our lives with the ability to tell precisely *how* the Spirit works. That is the problem with many older providential views of history. Those who held such views had a commendable sense of God's active role in history, but they also thought they could identify God's special providences. English Protestants, for instance, long held that God's special providence was manifested in the defeat of the Spanish Armada. Many adherents of popular Christianity today, despite an equally commendable sense of God's active work in their lives, show a similar confusion of the Holy Spirit's work and their own wishes or political aspirations.

The Holy Spirit works in mysterious ways. When we as Christians look at history, or study any human activity, we are dealing with a perplexing mix of divine and human agencies that is impossible to sort out. Historian Richard Lovelace suggests that this mix of the divine and the human is for the Christian scholar "as confusing as a football game in which half the players are invisible."[15] As scholars we are forced to deal with only those aspects of the picture for which human abilities are competent.

I find it helpful to think of this complex spiritual vision of reality as analogous to the fictional world constructed by J. R. Tolkien in *The Lord of the Rings.* Suppose we scholars thought of our understanding of things as equivalent to that of the Hobbits in Tolkien's world. The most important thing to take into account is that we are involved in a great spiritual struggle between forces of darkness and light. Beyond knowing that, we can understand these forces only imperfectly. Nonetheless as limited creatures we accept that our role is to do what we can to promote the cause of the light and to use all our talents where they may be helpful. As scholars, we might think of ourselves as something like map-readers on a mission the dimensions of which we cannot fully comprehend. Even so, we can try to do the best job we can of interpreting some technical down-to-earth matters that may contribute, in ways we do not fully understand, to the larger spiritual mission.[16]

If scholars saw themselves in such a role, they would not necessarily become more competent map-readers, but it might have a commendable impact on their *attitudes* toward their scholarship. On the one hand they might see that even seemingly modest scholarly tasks can be in the service of a higher cause, and on the other they would be less likely to have illusions about their scholarly vision. As we have seen, a tendency in modern scholarship is to aggrandize one's own perspective on reality. The larger tendency is to aggrandize scholarship itself. Anthropologists or geneticists may suggest that they have discovered the key to the origins of morality—or the origin of religion. Social scientists provide "expert" authority for new systems of morality. Historians may suggest that because everything has historical-cultural origins, all truth is relative to culture. Literary critics may argue that all of experience is a "text" subject to the authority of our interpretation. Astrophysicists may announce that if they can discover a "grand unified theory" they will, as Stephen Hawking put it, "Know the mind of God."[17] Christian scholars, while recognizing the value of scholarship, should also recognize its limitations. Rather than engendering intellectual arrogance, as unfortunately it often does, Christian belief should be a source of humility.

## THE HUMAN CONDITION

The inclusion of classic Christian conceptions of God in our picture of reality changes the ways we think about human beings. At the very least, it changes the relative importance that we assign to humans, human perceptions, and human creativity. Classic Christianity teaches us to love and value every other human more and ourselves less. We are not to have illusions about the human condition, however, or about human abilities to solve their own problems. These beliefs contrast sharply with the conceptions of humans that have dominated academic thought for the past century and a half. As we have already seen, with God out of the picture, humans loom as the ultimate creators of reality. The self, or perhaps the community or the nation, is inflated and absolutized. With consideration of the divine ruled out as unacademic or unprofessional, it has been widely assumed that humans can solve their own problems—as in the cult of psychotherapy, the cult of technological progress, or in the political cult of social amelioration. According to academic orthodoxy, if these problems cannot be solved by human means, then they cannot be solved at all. Cynicism is the only alternative, as we often see in academia today.

Classic Christianity, as Pascal suggests, sees human beings as both the crown of creation and the scum of the earth. As twentieth-century history illustrates so well, humans are fatally flawed creatures. In Reinhold Niebuhr's terms, this built-in flaw has a deeply ironic quality, in that we tend to turn our virtues into vices. We use our technological gifts to build horrible weapons of destruction. Our economic expertise, on which we build prosperity, also breeds uncontrollable greed so that we exploit the weak and destroy the environment. Our enlightened political systems and our hopes to create systems still more enlightened justify unprecedented warfare, enslavements, and exterminations of civilization populations. As Niebuhr puts it, a too confident sense of justice inevitably leads to injustice. These human vices are impossible for us to eradicate because they are built on our best qualities: our abilities to create, to choose, to build, to bring order and justice. Even our ability to love turns into inordinate love for our own family, community, interest group, or nation. At the heart of all our vices is the original sin, described in Genesis—the belief that we can be "as the gods," the unlimited creators and rulers of our own destiny.[18]

No one has framed the Christian account of the human condition more helpfully than St. Augustine in *The City of God*. Beginning with God as the Creator and central actor in human history, for Augustine the crucial question for humans is where they place their primary love. Christians are those who, by God's grace, are incorporated into the City of God. That community or civilization is built around the principle of love of God, the Creator. Loving God is a unifying experience. Augustine compares it to the experience of a vast audience in an amphitheater who are all drawn together by their shared admiration for a great actor. So those who respond to the love of God are drawn out of themselves to love not only

God but also his creatures. This is the principle on which the church is built, however imperfectly it may be realized in this life.

At the same time Christians live as pilgrims in the cities of the world. These civilizations are built on love of self and of the created things, rather than on love of the Creator. These worldly loves are the essence of the problem of the human condition, which we see manifested in our political, economic, social, and psychological relationships. Our loves are ultimately divisive, because people contend for the same limited objects.

Augustine's analysis of the human condition is far more complex. He is not saying simply that God is good, the world is bad, and that we therefore ought to love God and forsake the world. Christians are also subjects of particular governments, which have been ordained by God as relative goods. The nations of the world exist to prevent chaos, promote justice, and provide order that we all need. Christians should support them for the good that such order constitutes. Even though they are pilgrims whose ultimate allegiance is elsewhere, Christians also owe limited allegiance to the regimes of their earthly sojourns. At the same time Christians should have no illusions about political institutions. Ultimately they reflect the flaws of human nature and, despite the good they do, are founded on principles of self-love or self-interest. They are created by bloodshed and maintained by force.

Christians must keep in mind that their ultimate citizenship is in the higher "city" or civilization, one built on love to God and hence to his creation. To be part of this kingdom of God's love means one is united in the selflessness of Christ and so must renounce the in-born allegiances to self-interest and self love, which are the principles of the "earthly city" and have dominated history. The Christian's higher allegiance to the principles of the "city of God" should qualify all subordinate allegiances, whether to governments or other human institutions.

Augustine's model has many practical applications for Christian scholars. In fact, our entire account of Christian scholarship is built on an Augustinian base. The principle of a higher citizenship provides a framework for thinking about how Christians can be full-fledged participants in the secular academic institutions of the day, yet be free of illusions about those institutions. Rather than either accepting the current academic standards as ultimate, or rejecting them as hopelessly corrupt, Christian scholars can consider them valuable ad hoc principles for getting certain jobs done. At the same time, they will see in them what one finds in all human inventions, the tendency to absolutize the relative. Christians should thus be skeptical of the larger claims that periodically emanate from the academic community to the effect that we have now found the key to understanding reality or our constructions of it.

Political scientist Graham Walker summarizes well the implications of an Augustinian perspective in his study *Moral Foundations of Constitutional Thought*. An Augustinian way of thinking, he writes, "ultimately offers the sturdiest of reasons why the practices of law and government can—and should—remain concerned with less-than-ultimate matters."[19] The same might be said of the pragmatic dimensions of secular academia. It can—and should—remain concerned with less-than-ultimate matters. On that level it can do a very good job and like good government should receive our enthusiastic support. The problem arises when a secular pragmatic methodology that works well in a pluralistic setting is mistaken for a definitive account of reality. Like pragmatic government which denies its limits by wrapping itself in a cloak of sacred nationalism, so pragmatic academia tends to absolutize its relatively good methodology.

James W. Skillen in *Recharging the American Experiment: Principled Pluralism for Genuine Civic Community* offers a helpful overview of how Christian principles can bear on the question of building a genuinely pluralistic society. Skillen, executive director of the Center for Public Justice, emphasizes that for justice to prevail, governments have to attempt to treat every group with equity. Yet they are constantly under pressure to absolutize another set of interests or ideals, whether those of the market, the individual, the omnicompetent surrogate family and school, the race, or the nation itself. Often such concerns take on a virtually religious quality and lead to distortions of the relationships necessary to a just society. Skillen's work exemplifies how an explicitly Christian perspective can be brought to bear on some very practical issues. He also offers helpful principles for dealing with some of the questions addressed in this book, particularly those concerning how pluralistic structures ought to be related to confessional communities in a healthy society.[20]

As Skillen's work illustrates, the Augustinian theme of the human tendency to absolutize the relative can play an important role in Christian scholarship as it critiques the idols of the age. For instance, a fruitful classroom theme for Christian scholars since at least mid-century has been to identify the various "isms" that contend for our allegiance—nationalism, socialism, Marxism, liberalism, individualism, conservatism, scientism, subjectivism, objectivism, romanticism, feminism, ethnocentrism, relativism, intellectualism, anti-intellectualism, populism, elitism, materialism, consumerism, and so forth. Each of these "isms" represents some important value or insight, but each tends to absolutize one dimension of human experience and to subordinate all else to it. Christians need to be alert to these tendencies in human nature and culture and to respond to the spirits of the age with discrimination. The critique of "the transcendent self" in the previous chapter illustrates the sort of critical attitude toward current culture that should characterize Christian thought.

In order to avoid that "culture wars" mentality which, rather than loving one's "enemies," vilifies them, it is important for Christian scholars also to appreciate the positive value or insight that each of the "isms" of the age exaggerates. One of the reasons for Christian scholars to be working in the mainstream academy, rather than simply denouncing "the world" and staying in their own institutions, is that they can learn from the very spirit of the age they are ultimately opposing. Even though, á la Augustine, they may see humans as engaged in spiritual warfare, the weapons of their warfare must not be those of the earthly city.

Christians need also to be alert to the tendency of Christians themselves to absolutize the culturally relative, often in the name of Christ. Christian scholars who study the church or Christianity itself should recognize how Christian faith constantly becomes enmeshed with the cultural forces of the age. This adaptability of Christianity helps explain its worldwide impact; it also explains why it so often seems compromised. Not only do various "isms" reshape the church, but so do more impersonal forces such as those of the market, modern media, technology, or other forces associated with modernization. Accommodation to such forces is not always bad and is often necessary, but usually dangerous. The best education involves being not only critical, but self-critical. For that, the Christian perspective on the human condition and the deceptiveness of the human heart provides an excellent place to stand.

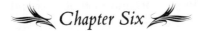# Chapter Six

# Building Academic Communities

Contemporary Christian scholarship will not realize its potential unless it can establish a strong institutional base. Isolated individuals in university culture can make impressive efforts here and there, but unless their voices are concerted, they will be lost in the general cacophony of the contemporary academy. The need for a book such as this one, pointing out what Christian scholarship looks like, is evidence that a passive, low-profile approach is not making much impact.

Scholars, like everyone else, depend on communities. If like-minded academics do not form their own sub-communities, then they will be dependent entirely on the communities that already exist. These, of course, have little place for inquiry concerning faith and learning. If such inquiry is to grow as a recognized part of contemporary academia, it must depend on institutions and networks which can sustain that enterprise.[1]

During the twentieth century the institutional infrastructures that might have supported high-level inquiry concerning faith and learning have steadily declined. At the opening of this century American denominations had hundreds of colleges and a number of universities with substantial religious identities. During the first half of the century, however, those progressive Protestants who set the standards for higher education typically assumed that there was no need for special religious identification because American cultural ideals and their broad religious ideals would coincide. Meanwhile, Catholics, conservative Protestants, and some ethnic Protestants were building their own educational systems. Mainline

Protestant denominationalists also retained many smaller colleges that provided religious alternatives to the dominant university culture. After mid-century, however, those who wanted to be fully accepted academically, especially mainline Protestants and Catholics, found that acceptance was easier if they jettisoned or subordinated their religious identities. Except on the peripheries of American higher education, institutional support for inquiry concerning faith and learning has continued to shrink.

There is a great need, then, to build and strengthen institutions that bring together scholars concerned with faith and learning. Such communities can be national or local. As described earlier, one of the most effective has been the Society of Christian Philosophers. Founded in 1978, it now includes some one thousand members and has been remarkably successful in reestablishing Christian perspectives in that field as acceptable, if not always welcome.[2] In my own experience the Institute for the Study of American Evangelicals (ISAE), an organization that includes a remarkable group of historians of North American Christianity, has played a similar role. The ISAE organizes conferences that bring together both Christian and non-Christian scholars from all over the English-speaking world and provides invaluable sustenance for scholarly exchange and encouragement. The Conference on Christianity and Literature, the Conference on Faith and History, and the American Scientific Affiliation also foster networks in history, literature and science, respectively. Each of these groups publishes its own journal and offers an organizational and intellectual base for cooperation and communication. Recently a number of e-mail networks have provided new resources for low-voltage contact among Christian scholars. As valuable as are these wider networks, however, more needs to be done at the local level where conversation can be more intense and ongoing.

One of the peculiarities of the Protestant contribution to the marginalization of religion in modern intellectual life has been that in the United States there are no Protestant research universities that approach anything like the first rank. Although there has been talk for two generations about founding a major Protestant university, the obstacles are formidable. So while Protestants support educational institutions at every other level, they have almost nothing to offer at the highest levels of scholarship and graduate training. At those levels, where a local community of likeminded scholars might be most important, there is the least to be found.

Nevertheless, there may be alternatives that would accomplish some of the same things. For instance, it should be possible to establish research institutes that, while encouraging first-rate scholarship in a particular area, would also explore the relationship of faith to learning. Such institutes might bring together some top-rank scholars who could also be affiliated with a major university. They could also include graduate students, offer post-graduate fellowships, and invite visiting scholars into the ongoing discussion. The Olin Center of the University of Chicago, best known as the domain of university critic Allan Bloom in his later years, provides a model from another ideological perspective. Relatively speaking, the costs would not be high and the possibilities for shaping an area of study would be considerable. What is needed is benefactors with vision and interested, qualified faculty.

Parallel programs could mobilize the resources of Catholic universities. Unlike American Protestants, Catholics still have a network of universities, some of which are at least academically competitive with the better universities. During the first half of the twentieth century when Protestants were abandoning the integration of Christianity in academic life, Catholics preserved a distinctive academic culture. Under the leadership of priests on their faculties, they concentrated on undergraduate education, teaching neo-Thomist principles in required courses and sustaining frequent campus worship. As a result, Catholic universities retained their religious identities, although they were not strong as research institutions. Since the 1950s they have become much more like their non-Catholic counterparts, often strengthening their graduate and research faculties and showing much more openness to diversity and academic freedom.[3] Today they still have definite Catholic identity, but its meaning is sharply debated.[4] Priests still leaven their faculties and they offer frequent opportunities for worship. With the demise of neo-Thomism as the intellectual norm, however, there is little agreement as to what Catholic intellectual life should look like even among those who want to see it sustained. Catholic universities have considerable potential, but it is a potential that will have to be mobilized if they are to continue to be havens for Christian intellectual life.

Catholic universities are ideally situated to establish institutes like those described above. Because Catholic universities today are committed to diversity among their faculties, university-wide requirements for sustaining Catholic intellectual life are difficult to implement. But centers that would explore the implications of Christian perspectives for various disciplines, arts, or practical applications of scholarship are a natural way to maintain a substantial Catholic component in a university's diversity.

Already there are quite a few such centers, dealing with a wide variety of topics such as the environment, peace, social concerns, business ethics, philosophy, education, and Catholic studies. Catholic universities would do well to develop the potentialities of such institutes to be primary agencies for exploring the implications of Christian perspectives for many pivotal university disciplines.

Another good way to build institutional bases that will sustain communities of Christian scholars is to strengthen the Christian academic dimensions of the hundreds of Christian liberal arts colleges, both Protestant and Catholic. These have retained varying degrees of religious identity as universities secularized. So one can find colleges across the entire spectrum of religious emphases.

Liberal arts colleges with both strong religious identities and some openness to the larger academic community are in the best position to encourage serious Christian academic discourse. These, however, like Catholic universities, face serious pressures to abandon such discourse entirely in order to conform to the dominant standards of the research universities. As we have seen, despite a tradition of diversity, American academic life today is marked by a strong centripetal force toward conformity. "Excellence" has been defined by research universities in purely secular terms. In recent decades faculty members of many of the smaller liberal arts colleges as well have increasingly adopted such secular standards. Other pressures push in the same direction to conform. Accrediting agencies, demands for academic freedom, ideas of separation of church and state, market forces, or pressure from donors, students, or alumni may all push toward standardized and secularized norms. Often, even when schools retain a substantial church affiliation, most of what is taught in their classrooms, except for Bible or theology courses, is indistinguishable from what is taught in state universities.

The widespread emphasis on "values," popular since at least World War II, has contributed to this loss of religious identity, while making it more palatable. Nobody, of course, can be against values. That is just the problem, however. Every institution claims to stress values. The term by itself is vacuous. Everyone can endorse it because it has no clear meaning. Church-related institutions that affirm continuity with their religious heritage by talking of their emphasis on values are saying almost nothing. This was confirmed by a study by a sociologist, Allen Fisher, who looked at sixty-nine colleges affiliated with the Presbyterian Church in the U.S. Almost all of their catalogues mentioned their emphasis on values, often as an expression of their religious heritage. Fisher compared the course offerings of these colleges to other colleges with no religious affiliation and found that, with few exceptions, there was no apparent difference in what was being taught.[5]

Christian perspectives, as we have seen, can make some important difference in moral judgments, but the difference should be more than that. Undergraduate teaching is the heart of higher education, and it is in undergraduate classrooms that students must begin to explore the intellectual relationships between their theological commitments and everything else they are learning. Emphasis on values can, of course, be invaluable. But it depends on the values and the reasons for holding them or acting on them. Determining how those values relate to the rest of what one affirms and learns is, among other things, serious intellectual business. If that business is neglected in Christian undergraduate education then students are being short-changed and will be little prepared to relate their faith to the rest of their lives.

Stephen Carter has observed that the great problem with religion in the United States is not its neglect, but its trivialization. That is true of the undergraduate education of many church-related schools. While the religious heritage may be honored in various way and celebrated in worship, a very different message is being sent in the classrooms. That message is that religion is really a private affair and that when it comes to the important things of life, such as understanding the world, our culture, other cultures, how you should make a living—matters that have to do with "the real world"—one should make no reference to beliefs that in other contexts are said to be ultimate.

In order to counter such pressures, church-related institutions need vigorous programs to promote reflection on the implications of Christian perspectives. As a first step, they need to do some consciousness-raising about the possibility of Christian scholarship and its compatibility with academic excellence. Such consciousness-raising is essential to counteract the widespread assumption that academic conformity, including conforming to standards of secularity, is essential to academic excellence. They also need to educate the public, including the political public, on the legitimacy of intellectual inquiry that goes beyond the usual secular limits. They must emphasize that if Americans are truly concerned for a healthy diversity, they must encourage diversity *among* institutions as well as diversity *within* institutions.

Schools that have a Christian heritage must also take some concrete steps to counteract the pressure to conform to the secular standards of the dominant university culture. Historically, the crucial issue has been faculty hiring. Without at least some faculty committed to integrating faith and learning, no amount of administrative rhetoric can sustain the enterprise. Many church-related schools are so open in their hiring that they can have little hope of retaining any aspect of their religious heritage. Faculty who are attuned only to the standards of the national academic culture will continue to hire people like themselves, thus eventually obliterating loyalties to any distinctive religious heritage. It is just a matter of time.

One way to counter such trends is to develop hiring policies that target faculty who are concerned to relate their faith to their teaching and scholarship. A pro-active way to do this would be to endow chairs for extra faculty positions for scholars who would both be excellent in their field and provide leadership in the area of faith and learning. Instead of encouraging pious donors to finance a new steeple for the chapel, administrators might encourage the endowment of such a chair. In that way within the diversity of an institution its own religious heritage would continue to be ably represented.

An even simpler way to resist the trend toward secular academic conformity is to adopt faculty development programs that cultivate the Christian academic consciousness of faculty who are already seriously religious. Most church-related schools have many faculty who are personally pious but consider their religion a private affair and so do not relate it to their academic life. They have not been exposed to academic cultures where discussions of faith and learning are high-level intellectual concerns. Recently a number of programs have been developed to counter such deficiencies. The Lilly Endowment has sponsored a Fellows Program in the Humanities and the Arts, which is building a sizable national network of church-related colleges and universities "interested in exploring Christian understandings of the nature of the academic vocation." Centered at Valparaiso University, this program involves permanent faculty and junior and senior fellows who spend a year or more together working as a community of Christian scholars. The Lilly Endowment has also supported

*Collegium,* a summer institute program for graduate students and new faculty at Catholic colleges, which also cultivates reflection of the meaning of faith for an academic calling.[6] The Pew Charitable Trusts has sponsored some similar programs for summer faculty development among schools of evangelical Protestant heritage.

As these programs recognize, it is crucial for Christian scholarship to build for the future. Many otherwise viable suggestions for building institutes or funding chairs are thwarted by the lack of outstanding senior scholars who have worked though the issues of faith and learning. On the other hand, anyone who is familiar with the Christian networks among graduate students and younger faculty will recognize that many committed young people, especially from evangelical Protestant heritages, are embarking on academic careers. Like the student radicals of the 1960s who are now the tenured professors, these young people may be harbingers of a change in American academia that will come to fruition in the next generation. For that promise to be fulfilled, it will be important to mobilize these students and provide for them a vision of what Christian scholarship might mean.[7]

## CULTIVATING SPIRITUAL VIRTUES

Mobilizing Christian academics is not first of all an intellectual matter. The prior questions are always spiritual. In order to have Christians who take seriously their callings as Christian scholars, we must first have scholars shaped by deep spiritual commitments. Churches and families are likely to be the principal places where such commitments are cultivated, but schools or sub-communities of Christian scholars can play vital supporting roles. Communal worship, fellowship, intellectual camaraderie, as well as simple caring, are invaluable for building up each other in the faith.

It is especially important for Christian scholars to recognize that mainstream academic culture and spiritual virtues are often at odds. Our academic system rewards self-promotion and specialized scholarship and gives little encouragement to cultivation of virtues. Often there seems to be an inverse relationship between scholarly production and spiritual virtues.[8] That is not necessarily the case, however, as anyone who knew the scholar to whom this book is dedicated can testify.

One way to counter some of the dangers of academic life is to try to convert its potential vices into virtues. Even in technical work one ought to be keeping in mind how scholarship is part of a Christian vocation, a form of service to others. Further, while the dominant academic reward system tends to encourage isolation, self-absorption, and self-promotion, much of scholarly research and writing can be means of relating to others, communicating to others, and attempting to serve others by discovering or saying something worthwhile. Such ends are easily lost sight of, as any research scholar knows. If counteracting virtues are not cultivated, it is easy to be coopted by a system of sheer competitiveness which is producing far more specialized information than the world really needs and which has no coherent moral rationale.

The spiritual virtues of Christian scholars ought to be reflected in both their teaching and other scholarship. The "fruit of the Spirit," according to Scripture, "is love, joy, peace, patience, kindness, goodness, faithfulness, gentleness and self-control."[9] These traits ought to mark the lives and the works of Christian scholars. People are seldom convinced simply by arguments, although arguments can be important. Most often in academia people are convinced by a combination of intellect and character. We have all sat under revered teachers whose word we came to believe not only because of what they said but also because of who was saying it. Many of the best academics are scholars who seldom publish but whose combination of intellectual interests and personal virtues results in lives dedicated to teaching and to their students. While this book is primarily about the theoretical basis for the relationship of faith to learning, it is essential to remember that teaching is the most important way in which the fruit of our labor is conveyed.

The same Christian virtues that characterize the best teaching should be evident in published scholarship. For instance, respect for the views of others, even while standing up for one's own, should be apparent not only in personal classroom dynamics but in the indirect communication of publication. In teaching or in publication scholars should speak unequivocally for their best perception of the truth, but also with humble understanding of others who think them wrong. That is a delicate balance not always achieved. Nonetheless, it is a valuable ideal.

Often people's first reaction to hearing the suggestion that there should be more Christian scholarship is that the last thing we need is another set of partisan ideologues. Ideally, however, Christian scholarship should be of a different stripe. While the presentation of any viewpoint involves some partisanship and occasional polemic, Christian partisanship and polemic should also be tempered by Christian virtues. Christianity at its best teaches people that they stand not at the center of reality, but on the periphery along with everyone else. It teaches that we are not dependent on our own brilliance and insight, but on a revelation that appears foolish to many and whose source we are unable to comprehend. It teaches that humans are flawed and often self-deluded creatures and that Christians are not exceptions. Hence our scholarship should be marked not only by firm defenses of the insights we believe we have seen revealed by God, but also by a willingness to be critical of ourselves and our own traditions.

BEYOND THE ENLIGHTENMENT

One of the questions most frequently asked, especially at church-related schools, is whether the process of the secularization of higher education is not inexorable. Harvard started out as a Puritan college in the seventeenth century, but by the late nineteenth century was liberal and soon largely secular. Yale started in the eighteenth century and continued its Christian emphases until the early twentieth century. The University of Chicago was founded in the 1890s as a Baptist school, and Duke University was endowed in the 1920s as Methodist. Now, they have little to show for those heritages except divinity schools and huge chapels. Will not much the same thing inevitably happen to the University of Notre Dame, Baylor University, Calvin College, or to any school unless it is willing to renounce the educational mainstream altogether?

Perhaps so. We should not underestimate the forces that push for a more standardized and secularized culture. Modern technology provides many financial incentives to move in that direction. Perhaps the standards of our research universities will absorb all but those who doggedly resist not only secular culture but contemporary intellectual life generally. During the 1950s there were many programs to foster mainline Protestant concern for matters of faith and learning, but these have long since all but disappeared. Will not the same thing happen to current programs and those suggested?

Perhaps so, but there is one very large difference. We now live in a postenlightened age. By that I mean we live in an era in which the promise of the Enlightenment, which dominated cultural life for almost three centuries, is passé. While nearly everyone endorses the procedural accomplishments of enlightened liberal culture, such as democratic polity, equal opportunity, and scientific rationality, no longer can it be assumed that the further one moves in such enlightened directions, the better things will be. Especially important, it can no longer be assumed that if scientific models are applied to all of life the world will be a better place. Through much of the twentieth century it was plausible to argue—an argument almost universally compelling to leading academics—that with the spread of modern education, traditional religious beliefs would disappear or recede into the cultural backwaters. It was also plausible to claim that if humans could simply put together their concerted intelligence they could go a long way to resolving many perennial human problems. As late as the 1960s we all heard, as I did at an academic conference, that if we can put a person on the moon, then we ought to be able to solve the problems of poverty.

While enlightened liberal culture has made great accomplishments that ought to be preserved, it can no longer be said to be obvious, or even probable, that simply more of the same is the key to social improvement. No longer is it so easy to assume that if we just become more open and more tolerant we will all get along better. Openness and diversity, we have discovered, have their own orthodoxies and their own intolerance. Academic culture, where such ideals have been most in vogue, does not offer coherent ideals that can serve as a beacon of enlightenment in a world of prejudice. No longer is it widely compelling to say if only more people were educated into the most progressive ideals, the world would be a better place.

The crucial point for our purposes is that for academic communities there should no longer be the assumption that the move to embrace the more enlightened and more secular standards of the culture of the research university is a course to improvement. Church-related liberal arts colleges are finding that, having preserved some of their traditional ways, they are now offering more of what people are looking for in higher education and hence are ahead of the game. So we have to recognize that our old assumptions about what constitutes progress have changed—or should change.

Despite nearly three centuries in which it was widely assumed (often correctly) that academic excellence went hand in hand with the lifting of religious restraints, there is good reason to consider alternatives. More openness to religious perspectives in the academic mainstream is not a total cure for its moral indeterminism. Nonetheless, it is time to face the fact, long suppressed in the highest intellectual circles, that a religiously diverse culture will be an intellectually richer culture. It is time to recognize that scholars and institutions who take the intellectual dimensions of their faith seriously can be responsible and creative participants in the highest levels of academic discourse.

So, despite the forces that continue to push for a homogeneous academic culture based exclusively on university research models, there is nothing that makes the long drift from the religious to the secular in higher education inevitable. There is good reason to hope that there will be increased consciousness of the nature of the issues and increasing numbers of scholars and institutions exploring them. If these trends continue, then there are good prospects that in the twenty-first century academia will be more open to perspectives that go beyond the Enlightenment on questions of religious faith.

# Getting Specific:
# A Readable Appendix

Those who are skeptical about the idea of Christian scholarship often ask for specific examples. A book like this, they may say, deals largely with generalities and lacks sufficient concreteness. Sympathetic observers sometimes make the same point. They may be open to pursuing Christian scholarship, but want to see some models.

If readers will survey the notes in this volume as well as the works mentioned in the text, they will find quite a few such examples. Moreover, it is not difficult to name works by a number of impressive scholars in most fields. One need only look at the lists of publications of scholars such as William Alston, Alasdair MacIntyre, Alvin Plantinga, Charles Taylor, and Nicholas Wolterstorff in philosophy; or Herbert Butterfield, Christopher Dawson, E. Harris Harbison, Nathan Hatch, Mark Noll, George Rawlyk, Harry Stout, James Turner, Dale Van Kley in history;[1] Stephen Carter, Jean Elshtain, Mary Ann Glendon, and James Noonan in political and legal theory; or Robert Bellah, Peter Berger, Jacques Ellul, and Robert Wuthnow in sociology (to name only a few fields) to be assured that there *is* first-rate scholarship that implicitly or explicitly reflects discernible and substantial Christian perspectives.[2] Not being a polymath, I am not going to attempt anything like a comprehensive list of examples. Rather, for those who still might say that there is little evidence that there could be a wide-ranging and substantial Christian scholarship, I think I can here furnish enough *different kinds* of examples to put that claim to rest. For others who wish to think more about how Christian perspectives might operate, these examples should be useful for seeing the kind of thing that is being done.

Although there are a number of rich traditions of Christian thought, one of the peculiarities of the past twenty-five years is that much of the interest in self-consciously Christian scholarship has been generated within the evangelical community, which is often assumed to be anti-intellectual. At the same time interest in explicitly relating faith to scholarship among mainline Protestants has declined. Catholic scholars remain among the important contributors, although since the opening up of the Catholic Church after Vatican II and the end of the dominance of the neo-Thomas synthesis, many Catholics who are scholars have reacted against the idea of developing specifically Catholic (or Christian) scholarship.[3] Even among the Protestant evangelicals, as Mark Noll has detailed in *The Scandal of the Evangelical Mind,* interest in serious Christian scholarship is found only among a minority of the many groups to whom the term "evangelical" may refer.[4]

Nevertheless, there has been a mini-renaissance of evangelical scholarship, and since this is what I know best, it is where I find most of my examples. Probably the most accessible reference for such works, including books and journals mostly by evangelical and other Christian writers, is "A Bibliography We Can't Live Without," in Brian J. Walsh and J. Richard Middleton, *The Transforming Vision: Shaping a Christian World View,* reprinted in James W. Sire, *Discipleship of the Mind.*[5] This bibliography of more than 150 books, while not claiming to be comprehensive, provides enough examples in just about every field of the arts and sciences to satisfy any skeptic that there is such a thing as Christian scholarship. The volumes by Walsh and Middleton and by Sire are also among several that are helpful in describing the ideal of Christian scholarship.[6] For overviews of how the ideal might work in particular fields, a good place to start is the series of books on various disciplines (including sociology, psychology, history, literature, music, biology, and business) sponsored by the Christian College Coalition.[7] Many other Christian scholars are working on projects that are not simply exploring first principles but applying some dimension of a Christian agenda to practical work in their field. One quick way to gain a sense of the scope and quality of such efforts is to peruse the past volumes of *Christian Scholar's Review.* Though not as well known or as widely circulated as it should be, this quarterly interdisciplinary journal includes not only critical reviews, but also excellent examples of how Christian perspectives may be applied in fields from the sciences to the arts.[8] A number of Christian academic organizations also publish significant journals. Prominent among these journals are the *Journal of the American Scientific Affiliation, Faith and Philosophy, Christianity and Literature,* and *Fides et Historia.*[9] *Books and Culture: A Christian Review* and *First Things* are more popular efforts to provide faith-informed commentary on contemporary culture.

For our present purposes, perhaps a useful way to illustrate how Christian perspectives operate in a variety of specific cases is to report on a conference I attended about the same time I was concluding this volume. Each summer "The Pew Evangelical Scholars Program" holds a brief conference to hear progress reports from recipients of research fellowships to promote Christian scholarship. The previous year I had sat on the board that chose from among over 250 applicants fourteen to be funded by the Pew Charitable Trusts. The term "evangelical" in the title of the program is interpreted broadly, so as to include Catholic, Orthodox, and mainline Protestants who can affirm that term. We were looking for scholarship that had some perceptibly Christian dimensions, in theology, the humanities, and the social sciences.

Since for our purposes the relevance of Christian perspectives to scholarship outside of theology itself is at issue, I shall mention just the ten projects in the humanities and social sciences. A brief description of each of these will show how Christian perspectives shape a variety of scholarly agendas.

Eleonore Stump is dealing with the philosophy of Thomas Aquinas, a topic that has proven intellectually fruitful almost as long as there have been universities. Stump, who teaches at St. Louis University, has been a prominent figure in the Society of Christian Philosophers. Her expertise is not only in medieval thought but in current issues regarding Christianity and contemporary philosophy, so this work is a search for new insights on perennial themes.

Anthony Low, Professor of English at New York University, is working on a book on "Umpire Conscience: The Transformation of the Self in Seventeenth-Century Literature." In earlier Western culture, he points out, one answered the question of "Who am I?" largely by looking at external sources, such as family, social standing, or relation to the church and God.

In modern conceptions, one increasingly evaluates the self by looking for inner meaning. In seventeenth-century literature one can see the conflict between these two views.

James Bradley, a historian at Fuller Theological Seminary, is viewing eighteenth-century England from a different angle. Bradley notes that current postmodern critiques of the Enlightenment usually assume that Christian thought lost out in the eighteenth century because of its inability to meet the demands of the modern world. In fact, Bradley argues, there are many positive eighteenth-century Christian contributions to modern thought that have since been obscured and are now worth re-exploring.

Luis Martínez-Fernández, Professor of Puerto Rican and Hispanic Caribbean Studies at Rutgers University, also works on correcting historical prejudices, a theme that leads into much territory fruitful for Christian scholarship. According to Martínez-Fernández, there has been an anti-Protestant bias in most Caribbean studies. His own study of nineteenth-century Protestant missions argues that, in fact, the missions were not usually oppressive, as is often supposed, but rather were often politically progressive.

Karla Poewe, an anthropologist at the University of Calgary, is working on a similar corrective. The literature of the field of anthropology almost universally assumes that missionaries represented culturally retrogressive and oppressive interests. Looking at German materials, Poewe shows that early German anthropology was long dependent on learned contributions of missionary observers who had far more nuanced views of other cultures than has typically been taken for granted.

R. Bruce Mullin, an historian at North Carolina State University, helps correct yet another prejudice of twentieth-century scholarship. In his forthcoming study of "Miracles and the Modern Religious Imagination," Mullin shows that intellectuals who at the turn of the past century claimed that belief in miracles was passé were mistaking their own experience for reality. Not only were new popular religious groups re-emphasizing the miraculous; but even among some prominent Protestant intellectuals there was a new openness to belief that the age of miracles had not ended with the biblical era. Like many other recent studies, Mullin drives another stake into the twentieth-century academic assumption that the modern age inexorably breeds secularization and the disenchantment of reality.

Andrew M. Manis, Professor of Religion at Averett College, is attempting to broaden our understanding of the Christian contributions to the civil rights movement. To date, almost all such attention has been focused on Martin Luther King. Manis is working on a biography of Fred Shuttlesworth, a civil rights organizer in Birmingham, Alabama. Shuttlesworth's more populist style blended traditional African-American spirituality with militant political concerns.[10]

Thomas W. Heilke, a political scientist at the University of Kansas, finds another source for positive Christian contributions to political thought. By looking at Anabaptist sources, he provides fresh angles of vision for dealing with some of the troubling problems arising from the moral indeterminism of modern democracy.

Another social scientist, Janel Curry-Roper, a geographer at Central College in Iowa, brings Christian insights to bear in considering agricultural policy. Modern society is unable to arrive at intelligible goals for its agricultural programs because it deals either with individuals or with undifferentiated groups, as in social surveys. Curry-Roper, informed by some motifs in Christian social thought, argues that the community should be viewed as the building-block of society. With that in mind, she has studied the religiously informed worldviews of various ethnic farming communities in Iowa to see how these worldviews bear on views of natural resource management.

Clifford Christians, Professor of Communications at the University of Illinois, looks at the underlying crisis in authority in the social sciences. Societies need some unquestionable standards that everyone can agree on, such as it is not acceptable to have open season on killing other human beings. Modern social science has been unable and often unwilling to provide a basis for a such standards, even when it takes them for granted. As postmodernist attacks have shown, it is impossible to establish any normative standards on the basis of pure naturalism. Christians suggests that the alternative has to be sought not in reason alone, but rather on the basis of faith in a created order that is not dependent on us for its standards.

Alan Jacobs looks at one individual's confrontation with the inability of modern thought to provide moral norms. Jacobs, who teaches English at

Wheaton College in Illinois, is studying the conversion to Christianity of W. H. Auden in the years from 1939 to 1944. Rejecting earlier faith in Freudianism, Marxism, and aesthetic fulfillment of the autonomous self, Auden came to believe that these modern formulae were empty in the face of world and personal crisis. Auden's turn to Christianity did not lead to a creative decline, but (as we have seen earlier) to profound insights into the modern predicament.

Let me broaden the range of illustrations by citing one more set of examples with which I am particularly familiar. Among the most ambitious efforts that I know of to cover a variety of academic topics were the yearly interdisciplinary projects sponsored by the Calvin Center for Christian Scholarship at Calvin College from the late 1970s until the early 1990s. Out of these emerged a series of substantial volumes on topics including Christianity's relationship to many current issues, such as stewardship of the environment, education, faith and reason, sociology, hermeneutics, technology, psychology, creation and Creation Science, economics, health and medical practice, justice in Central America, Protestantism in Latin America, youth culture, and gender reconciliation. Furthermore, a compilation of the works of the fellows at the Calvin Center (which includes both Calvin faculty and visiting fellows for each year), would constitute a formidable bibliography of Christian scholarship on a wide range of topics.[11]

Many books are to an extent autobiographical. Certainly this one is. It reflects over twenty years of participation at Calvin College in a community that was intellectually first-rate, deeply committed to Christian scholarship, and remarkably productive for an undergraduate liberal arts college. Conventional wisdom today says that intellectual vitality can be attained only in diverse intellectual settings. The level of scholarship attained at Calvin College, a theologically homogeneous community, during the past forty years is evidence to the contrary. The fact is a true community of scholars can operate in a homogeneous setting where a spirit of intellectual inquiry is encouraged. One does not have to go back to square one and argue first principles every time one has a substantial exchange with colleagues. There are plenty of differences of opinion, but they can be debated beyond the elementary level.

In the light of my experience in that community, the question that has motivated this book is why Christian scholarship has such a low reputation in the rest of the academic community. Why is such scholarship thought to be impossible, nonsensical, or non-existent? Why is it not practiced more widely in other Christian institutions that appear to have commitments both to Christianity and to excellent scholarship? Why do not more scholars who are Christian think deeply about the relevance of faith to their scholarship? I hope this volume has helped to raise consciousness about these issues.

# Notes

## INTRODUCTION

1. All but the last three of these questions are borrowed from an address to the Pew Younger Scholars, June 1995, by my friend and former colleague, Nicholas Wolterstorff.

Wolterstorff's own publications are models of Christian scholarship and it may help to list them here to suggest the kind of thing I have in mind. His books include *Art in Action: A Christian Aesthetic* (Grand Rapids: William B. Eerdmans, 1980), *Divine Discourse: Philosophical Reflections on the Claim That God Speaks* (Cambridge: Cambridge Univ. Press, 1995), *Educating for Responsible Action* (Grand Rapids: CSI Publications, William B. Eerdmans, 1980), *Faith and Rationality: Reason and Belief in God,* edited with Alvin Plantinga (Notre Dame, Ind.: Univ. of Notre Dame Press, 1983), *John Locke and the Ethics of Belief* (New York: Cambridge Univ. Press, 1996), *Mind, World and the Entitlement to Believe,* The Gifford Lectures for 1994–95 (Cambridge: Cambridge Univ. Press, 1996), *On Universals: An Essay on Ontology* (Chicago: Univ. of Chicago Press, 1970), *Reason Within the Bounds of Religion* (1976; Grand Rapids: William B. Eerdmans, 1984), *Until Justice and Peace Embrace* (Grand Rapids: William B. Eerdmans, 1983), *Works and Worlds of Art* (Oxford: Clarendon Press, 1980).

2. Bruce Kuklick as reported by Carolyn J. Mooney, "Devout Professors on the Offensive," *Chronicle of Higher Education,* May 4, 1994, p. A18.

3. Letters to the editor, *Chronicle of Higher Education:* Alexander S. Holub, June 1, 1994, p. B5, Robert Primack, May 25, 1994, pp. B5–B6, William Matta, June 1, 1994, p. B4.

4. Kuklick, loc. cit., the quotation is the reporter's summary.

5. In a review of *The Soul of the University* Thomas Bender of New York University

argues that since many academics are Christians and some of them profess to be influenced by Christianity in their academic work, there is not the prejudice against Christianity that I allege. Bender bases his remarks on a survey of historians of the United States conducted by the Organization of American Historians which found that 14.8% of respondents from the United States listed religion as among their "allegiances or identities important to them as historians." About the same percentage listed the Bible as a major intellectual influence, putting it far ahead of any other particular book. I would interpret these statistics quite differently. Probably many of the 15% who see the Bible and religion as important teach at Christian colleges. If that is true, then my point stands that only a small percentage of academics in mainstream academia think to mention religion as a significant academic influence.

According to a survey in the early 1980s, 49% in the social sciences, 46% in the humanities, 41% in the biological sciences, and 37% in the physical sciences said they were indifferent or opposed to religion. That suggests both that there is indeed some hostility to religion in academia and that there are majorities who have at least some sympathy. If even a third to a half of these are fairly serious about their religious beliefs, we are left with a substantial minority of religious academics, even in the mainstream. So if the main question is self-censorship rather than discrimination against religious people, these statistics would support my point. Thomas Bender, "Putting Religion in its Place?," *Culturefront* (Fall 1994): 77–79. Cf. "A Statistical Summary of Survey Results," *Journal of American History* 81:32 (Dec. 1994): 1193, 1203. Survey as reported in Robert Wuthnow, *The Struggle for America's Soul* (Grand Rapids: William B. Eerdmans, 1989), 146–47, from Stephen Steinberg, *The Academic Melting Pot: Catholics and Jews in American Higher Education* (New York: McGraw Hill, 1974).

6. Peter Steinfels, "Universities Biased against Religion, Scholar Says," *New York Times,* Nov. 26, 1993, p. A22.

7. Despite this important point, in order to avoid confusion, I usually use "faith" in the more ordinary sense as referring to a specifically religious faith.

CHAPTER ONE

WHY CHRISTIAN PERSPECTIVES
ARE NOT WELCOMED

1. A former graduate student in New Testament studies at the same university reports: "I quickly learned that some religious teachers were actively indoctrinating undergraduates against the Bible. When I talked at length with one professor about it, he argued that 'academic freedom' meant that he could attack Christianity and Judaism, and grade down biblically conservative students, if he liked. At the same time, he argued that any teacher who publicly acknowledged that he or she believed in God should be fired." Craig Keener, letter to the editor, *InterVarsity Magazine* (Fall 1992): 2.

Such blatant prejudice is rare; but students from conservative backgrounds often report hostility toward their views.

2. In a news story on the subject in *CQ Researcher,* a representative of the American Association of University Professors (AAUP) was reported as saying that there was no good evidence of bias based on religion since the AAUP received few complaints of such. What he did not take into account was the self-censorship that results in an academic culture where it is taken for granted that explicit religious reference is in bad taste. "Are American Colleges Biased Against Religion . . . Or Are They Receptive to the Study of Religion?," *CQ Researcher* IV: 7 (Feb. 18, 1994): 162–63.

3. In addition to *The Soul of the American University: From Protestant Establishment to Established Nonbelief* (New York: Oxford Univ. Press, 1994) see the essays in George M. Marsden and Bradley J. Longfield, eds., *The Secularization of the Academy* (New York: Oxford Univ. Press, 1992).

4. These themes are developed in James Turner, *Without God, Without Creed: The Origins of Unbelief in America* (Baltimore: Johns Hopkins Univ. Press, 1985), and in George M. Marsden, *Understanding Fundamentalism and Evangelicalism* (Grand Rapids: William B. Eerdmans, 1991), ch. 5, "The Evangelical Love Affair with Enlightenment Science," 122–52.

5. Gertrude Himmelfarb, "The Christian University: A Call to Counterrevolution," emphasizes that "Indeed, it was the idea of 'culture'—a secular, rational, cosmopolitan, liberal (in the nonpolitical sense of the word) culture—far more than the idea of 'science,' that lay behind the secularization of the University in the late-nineteenth and early-twentieth centuries." *First Things* 59 (Jan. 1996): 16. James M. Turner makes a similar point in "Secularization and Sacralization: Speculations on Some Religious Origins of the Secular Humanities Curriculum, 1850–1900," in Marsden and Longfield, eds., *Secularization of the Academy,* 74–106.

6. D. G. Hart, "Faith and Learning in the Age of the University: American Learning and the Problem of Religious Studies," in Marsden and Longfield, eds., *Secularization of the Academy,* 195–233.

7. Philip Gleason, *Speaking of Diversity: Language and Ethnicity in Twentieth-Century America* (Baltimore: Johns Hopkins Univ. Press, 1992), provides an excellent discussion of these issues.

8. This is a major theme of Christopher Jencks and David Riesman, *The Academic Revolution* (1968; Chicago: Univ. of Chicago Press, 1977).

9. Stephen L. Carter, *The Culture of Disbelief: How American Law and Politics Trivialize Religious Devotion* (New York: Basic Books, 1993), passim.

10. Alasdair MacIntyre, *Three Rival Versions of Moral Enquiry: Encyclopaedia, Genealogy, and Tradition.* (Notre Dame, Ind.: Univ. of Notre Dame Press, 1990), 19, cf. 9–31.

11. During the 1950s there was a substantial campaign led by mainline Protestants to promote such perspectives. See Douglas Sloan, *Faith and Knowledge: Mainline Protestantism and Twentieth-Century American Higher Education* (Philadelphia: Westminster Press, 1994). Sloan shows how the mainline Protestant project of keeping a place for religion

in higher education was weakened by its two-layered view of truth that separated the realm of faith from the realm of scientifically based knowledge.

12. Hart, "Faith and Learning," in Marsden and Longfield, eds., *Secularization of the Academy*, 195–233.

13. "Are American Colleges Biased?," 162–63.

Understandably, proponents of religious studies may also prefer to put the question this way. Barbara DeConcini, the executive director of the American Academy of Religion, in a letter to the editor, *New York Times Book Review,* May 15, 1994, p. 39, regarding a review of *The Soul of the American University* cited the growth of religious studies as counterevidence to what she took to be my complaint. DeConcini's defense may have been prompted by the language of the reviewer, John Patrick Diggins, in his review, *New York Times Book Review,* April 17, 1994, p. 25, where he speaks of "religion" being "driven from campus" when referring to lack of explicit religious perspectives in classrooms. Some religious studies professors in mainline positions do represent the perspectives of particular religions, but the trend of recent decades does seem to be toward more detached "history of religions" approaches. Complicating debate on this subject is also the fact that theologically more traditional versions of Christianity have seldom had much representation on mainline university religion faculties.

14. John Courtney Murray, S.J., used this term in the 1950s, and it was legally recognized in 1961 when Justice Hugo L. Black wrote in a 1961 Supreme Court Decision (Supreme Court Case 367 U. S., at p. 495): "Among religions in this country which do not teach what would generally be considered a belief in the existence of God are Buddhism, Taoism, Ethical Culture, Secular Humanism and others." Martin Marty, *The New Shape of American Religion* (New York: Harper and Row, 1958), 76–80, noted Murray's use of the term and went on to point out that this "secular and humanistic faith" was often associated with a vaguely theistic faith in the American way of life and had "'an established church' in the field of public education."

CHAPTER TWO

THE ARGUMENTS FOR SILENCE

1. Bernard Rosen, as reported by Jeff Grabmeier, "Christian Professors, Public University," *Ohio State Quest* (Summer 1994): 15–16. Note similar comments in letters to the *Chronicle of Higher Education,* quoted in the introduction.

2. Peter Novick, *That Noble Dream: The "Objectivity Question" and the American Historical Profession* (Cambridge, Eng.: Cambridge Univ. Press, 1988), describes the changing views on this subject among American historians.

3. This is particularly clear, for instance, in John Dewey, *The Reconstruction of Philosophy* (New York: Henry Holt, 1920).

4. Novick, *That Noble Dream, passim.*

5. These higher ways of knowing often included something like the religious imagination as well, as discussed in Chapter One.

6. Alvin Plantinga, *The Twin Pillars of Christian Scholarship,* the Stob Lectures of Calvin College and Seminary, 1989–90 (Grand Rapids, Mich.: Calvin College and Seminary, 1990), esp. 14–17. Plantinga's categories are useful as shorthand "ideal types" representing large philosophical trends that have undercut traditional Christian beliefs. Such broad categories, however, also tend to blur the nuances in such philosophies, and the sweeping suggestion that these outlooks are antithetical to Christian thought can be confusing historically. For instance, something a lot like creative anti-realism has, rightly or wrongly, often been used to support some versions of Christian belief.

7. Two recent collections exemplifying these remarkable developments are Kelly James Clark, ed., *Philosophers Who Believe: The Spiritual Journeys of 11 Leading Thinkers* (Downers Grove: InterVarsity Press, 1993), and Thomas V. Morris, *God and the Philosophers; The Reconciliation of Faith and Reason* (New York: Oxford Univ. Press, 1994).

8. Their message is, of course, vigorously resisted by many other philosophers, as the comments quoted at the opening of this chapter suggest.

9. Randall Balmer, "Response to George Marsden," presented at the forum on "Academic Freedom and Committed Scholarship: The 1992 ASCH Presidential Address Revisited," American Society of Church History meetings, Jan. 8, 1994.

10. For more on this theme, see George M. Marsden, *Fundamentalism and American Culture: The Shaping of Twentieth-Century Evangelicalism, 1870–1925* (New York: Oxford Univ. Press, 1980) and *Understanding Fundamentalism and Evangelicalism* (Grand Rapids: William B. Eerdmans, 1991).

11. "Framework Regarding Prevention of Harassment and Discrimination in Ontario Universities," Ministry of Education and Training, Ontario, Canada (ca. 1993). For some of the public controversy, see the following editorials: Peter Stockland, "Thumper Rabbit Goes to College in Ontario," *Ottawa Sun,* Feb. 16, 1994; Peter Stockland, "NDP's Brave New World," *Ottawa Sun,* Feb. 20, 1994; and Robert Fulford, "The Curious Unfolding of Zero Tolerance," *Toronto Globe and Mail,* Feb. 23, 1994. I am also indebted to Professor David Jeffrey of the University of Ottawa for his account as a participant in the outcry against the rules.

12. See George Marsden, *The Soul of the American University: From Protestant Establishment to Established Nonbelief* (New York: Oxford Univ. Press), 292–316, 433–35.

13. Dinesh D'Souza, *Illiberal Education: The Politics of Race and Sex on Campus* (New York: Free Press, 1991); Roger Kimball, *Tenured Radicals: How Politics Has Corrupted Higher Education* (New York: Harper and Row, 1990); and Richard Bernstein, *Dictatorship of Virtue: How the Battle over Multiculturalism Is Reshaping Our Schools, Our Countries, Our Lives* (New York: Vintage Books, 1994), among others, provide lots of anecdotal evidence on this score.

14. "Background: School Bible Disputes," *CQ Researcher* (Feb. 18, 1994): 153–56, provides a summary of the court developments. Phillip Johnson, "Why the Court's

Squeezed Lemon," *Books and Culture* I:2 (Nov./Dec. 1995): 5–6, provides a brief interpretive introduction to some recent developments.

15. Warren A. Nord, *Religion and American Education: Rethinking a National Dilemma* (Chapel Hill: Univ. of North Carolina Press, 1995), provides the most complete and balanced discussion of these issues.

16. They do present some arguments about how a young earth and a worldwide flood might fit with the evidence, but no one would be likely to give much credit to such arguments unless they were already convinced by a literalist reading of the Bible that the earth cannot be very old.

For a conservative Christian critique, see Clarence Menninga, Howard Van Till, and Davis Young, eds., *Science Held Hostage: What's Wrong with Creation Science and Evolutionism* (Downers Grove, Ill.: InterVarsity Press, 1988).

17. Franky Schaeffer, *Bad News for Modern Man: An Agenda for Christian Activism* (Westchester, Ill.: Crossway Books, 1984), 83.

18. The change in the Court's disposition is indicated in its 1995 ruling in *Rosenberger v. Rector and Visitors of University of Virginia.* As the dissent noted in this 5 to 4 decision, the majority does not mention the Lemon test at all and argues the issue on free-speech grounds rather than in terms of strict separation of religion from the state. Although the implications for the classroom are not at all clear, the decision raises the prospect, as one critic puts it, that "[i]n practical terms, *Rosenberger* makes it virtually impossible for a university to make defensible distinctions between religious and non-religious activities. . . ." Lawrence White, "The Profound Consequences of the 'Rosenberger' Ruling." *Chronicle of Higher Education,* July 14, 1995, p. B2. See also *Chronicle of Higher Education,* July 7, 1995, pp. A24–A33, for news summary and texts of decision and dissent.

CHAPTER THREE

CHRISTIAN SCHOLARSHIP AND THE RULES
OF THE ACADEMIC GAME

1. Stanley Fish, "Why We Can't All Just Get Along," *First Things* 60 (Feb. 1996), 21.

2. Thomas G. Alexander, R. Scott Appleby, and Amanda Porterfield each raised essentially sympathetic versions of this question, at the forum on "Academic Freedom and Committed Scholarship: The 1992 ASCH Presidential Address Revisited," American Society of Church History meetings, Jan. 8, 1994.

3. William James, *Pragmatism and the Meaning of Truth* (Cambridge: Harvard Univ. Press, 1978), 32. I am grateful to Amanda Porterfield for bringing this passage to my attention in the discussion just cited.

4. I am using "pragmatism" here for lack of a better term and not in any specialized philosophical sense. I am thinking of the rules that are necessary for pluralistic academic institutions to work equitably. I am using "liberal" not in the political sense as opposed to "conservative," but in the sense of a modern culture and polity such as is found in the United States.

5. See, for instance, Dewey's list of "goods" in John Dewey, *A Common Faith* (New Haven: Yale Univ. Press, 1934), 51.

Thomas Bender, in a letter to the author, March 23, 1995, argues that Dewey would have been open to something like the approach I am now describing. If that is true, so much the better for my argument. Nonetheless, I think that *in practice* the spiritual descendants of Dewey have tended to dismiss traditional religious viewpoints as not worthy of serious academic consideration.

6. I realize, of course, that there are lots of hard cases in which people using scientific procedures have legitimate differences over what constitutes "the facts" as Michael Polanyi and Thomas Kuhn have pointed out. Also, "facts" are never entirely independent from the interpretive systems in which we view them. Nonetheless, in judging many topics there remain lots of common standards on which almost everyone can agree for all practical purposes.

7. Leo P. Ribuffo suggests this point when he asks whether I would be comfortable with such a dispensationalist in "God and Man at Harvard, Yale, Princeton, Berkeley, etc." (review of Marsden, *The Soul of the American University*), *Reviews in American History* 32:1 (March 1995): 174–75.

8. This is not to say that political concerns might not be legitimate grounds for excluding some religiously based views from the mainstream. If, for instance, one taught that God has ordained a hierarchy of races and racial separatism, those beliefs will be excluded both by law and by an overwhelming consensus. Such rules keep changing, however, and so raise some hard questions so far as religious belief is concerned. What of Muslim, Mormon, or fundamentalist views of women? Or Catholic views of homosexuality? Are they in the same class as racist views? On the other hand, is excluding these views a kind of religious prejudice? Regardless of how these issues are decided, however, the important thing to notice is that the primary issue at stake is not whether a view has a religious basis, but rather has to do with the political implications of the views, whatever their origins.

9. Nicholas Wolterstorff, *Reason Within the Bounds of Religion* (1976; Grand Rapids: William B. Eerdmans, 1984). Wolterstorff himself makes a distinction between "control belief" and "background beliefs," including in the latter category less controversial beliefs (such as that I am essentially the same person today as I was yesterday). "Control beliefs," in his terminology, also do not have to remain in the background. What I am talking about here might be more precisely called "background control beliefs."

10. Thomas Bender, "Putting Religion in Its Place" (review of Marsden, *The Soul of the American University*), *CultureFront* 3:3 (Fall 1994): 78–79.

11. Cf. Stanley Hauerwas and William Willimon, *Resident Aliens: A Provocative Christian Assessment of Culture and Ministry for People Who Know That Something Is Wrong* (Nashville: Abingdon, 1989). Hauerwas in a host of books insists on maintaining that Christian communities should take a prophetic stance over against liberal culture rather than, as is here being attempted, developing accounts of how the "aliens" ought to live with respect to the rules of the host culture and work to make them relatively better.

12. Fish, "Why We Can't All Just Get Along."

## CHAPTER FOUR
### WHAT DIFFERENCE COULD IT POSSIBLY MAKE?

1. Bruce Kuklick, Review of Marsden, *The Soul of the American University,* in *Method & Theory in the Study of Religion* 8-1 (1996), 82.

2. On Calvin's scholarship, see the Appendix and its concluding note.

3. Ronald A. Fagan and Raymond G. DeVries, "The Practices of Sociology at Christian Liberal Arts Colleges and Universities," *American Sociologist* (Summer 1994): 21–39, document that the great majority of sociologists at Christian liberal arts colleges (selected from the Christian College Coalition) profess to relate their faith to their work as sociologists. A typical comment is:

> We ask the students to examine the theoretical perspectives in the light of their Christian perspectives and to accept what is acceptable. We suggest that they not blindly accept the social order of things, but to critically evaluate each issue over against their understanding of God's will for their lives and to operate accordingly. (32)

Apropos some of the topics in earlier chapters, Fagan and DeVries report, "When asked how the majority of sociologists felt about Christian sociologists 84% said the majority of sociologists view them as inferior or view them poorly." (33)

4. David A. Hollinger, "From Protestant Culture to Religious Pluralism," paper presented to Wingspread Conference on the History of American Protestantism, Racine, Wisconsin, October 1993, p. 33.

Hollinger may also have in mind that, in contrast to feminism, Christianity has not produced much in the line of innovative analytic categories. If that is his meaning, it needs to be said that, while Christianity in its marginalized position has not contributed much to the *common* stock of analytic devices in the past century, its earlier history furnishes many examples of contributions to Western intellectual methods and traditions. Scholars often see some current modes of thought as secularized pieces of Christian tradition, but then they seem to assume that there is no potential for similar contributions in the future.

In fact, there have been some significant Christian contributions even in the twentieth century to the common stock of ways of looking at things. Some examples that come to mind are Reinhold Niebuhr's analysis of the human condition (which was popular among a number of "atheists for Niebuhr") and just-war theory during the Vietnam War era. The principle of subsidiarity (from Catholic social encyclicals) may have contributed as well to political thinkers wrestling with the issues surrounding development of the Common Market into the European Community. (I am indebted to James Turner for most of this comment.)

5. Van Kley's synthesis, culminating three decades of research and publication on this topic, is *The Religious Origins of the French Revolution: From Calvin to the Civil Constitution, 1560–1791* (New Haven: Yale Univ. Press, 1996).

6. Robert Wuthnow, "Living the Question," in *Christianity in the Twenty-First Century: Reflections on the Challenges Ahead* (New York: Oxford Univ. Press, 1993), 209, 211, 212.

7. Mark Noll, *The Scandal of the Evangelical Mind* (Grand Rapids: William B. Eerdmans, 1994).

8. Robert Wuthnow, "The Scandal of the Evangelical Mind: A Symposium," *First Things* 51 (March 1995): 40–41.

9. In the same symposium Grant Wacker, another Christian scholar (and my close friend), laments the idea that evangelicals should try "to establish a Christian view of everything" and observes that most of Mark Noll's own scholarship meets the "technical protocols of historical scholarship that are pretty much applicable to everyone in the profession." Wacker, *First Things* 51 (March 1995): 36.

10. For instance, Paul Boyer, "Invisible Saints? Religion in American History Textbooks, Survey Course, and Historical Scholarship," Conference on Faith and History, Oct. 7, 1994, raises such points. I am grateful to Boyer, who has been a congenial critic and correspondent, for furnishing a copy of his draft for this presentation.

11. There will still be subtle differences. For instance, the set of questions and agendas that shapes a Marxist's scholarship is likely to be quite different from the non-Marxist's set. So even though many particular academic questions may seem to be the same for Marxist and non-Marxist scholars, they will be related to other questions and agendas that put them into a different framework. In that sense the questions and agendas may be different (as, for instance, their relative importance in relation to one's larger scale of values); but for practical purposes the difference will not be apparent. So also it is likely that committed Christians who are serious about their scholarship will ask distinctively Christian sets of questions and place their answers in a different context. Such distinctions are subtle, however, and even friendly observers are often misled, so it may not be helpful to emphasize them.

12. Harry S. Stout, "Theological Commitment and American Religious History," *Theological Education* (Spring 1989): 44–59 (quotations from 55, 55–56, and 58). For the discussion of Stout's *The Divine Dramatist*, see "Evangelicals and the Writing of

History," which reprints a letter to the editor from Stout to the *Banner of Truth* magazine, which had criticized him, and a response from its editor, Iain H. Murray, *Evangelical Studies Bulletin* 12:1 (Spring 1995): 6–9.

13. Lee Hardy, "Christian Education and the Postmodern Reconfiguration of Public Space," *The Cresset* (June 1993): 37. This is a review essay on *Schooling Christians: "Holy Experiments" in American Education*, Stanley Hauerwas and John H. Westerhoff, eds. (Grand Rapids: William B. Eerdmans, 1992). *Schooling Christians* includes a number of essays that make this point cogently.

14. *Three Rival Versions of Moral Enquiry: Encyclopaedia, Genealogy, and Tradition* (Notre Dame, Ind.: Univ. of Notre Dame Press, 1990).

15. Nicholas Wolterstorff, "The Schools We Deserve," in Hauerwas and Westerhoff, eds., *Schooling Christians*, 3–28.

16. Similar neglect of religion has been documented in other fields. For instance, Paul G. Schervish, "Wealth and the Spiritual Secret of Money," in *Faith and Philanthropy in America: Exploring the Role of Religion in America's Voluntary Sector*, Robert Wuthnow and Virginia A. Hodgkinson, eds. (San Francisco: Jossey-Bass, 1990), 63–90, shows that up to that time little of the literature on philanthropy had looked at religious motivations. Robert D. Woodberry, "Ideology and Social Movements," graduate paper in sociology, University of Notre Dame, 1995, reports that of four reviews of the literature on prosocial behavior/moral development, none looks at religious belief as an independent variable.

Kimberly A. Sherrill and David B. Larson, "The Anti-Tenure Factor in Religious Research in Clinical Epidemiology and Aging," 149–77, and David B. Larson, Kimberley A. Sherrill, and John S. Lyons, "Neglect and Misuse of the R. Word: Systematic Reviews of Religious Measures in Health, Mental Health, and Aging," 178–95, in *Religion in Aging and Health: Theoretical Foundations and Methodological Frontier*, Jeffrey S. Levin, ed. (Thousand Oaks: Sage, 1994), document the lack of attention to religious faith as an independent variable in the literature on aging. I am indebted to Robert Woodberry for these references.

17. Carl Sagan, *Cosmos* (New York: Random House, 1980), 4.

18. Donald M. MacKay, *The Clockwork Image: A Christian Perspective on Science* (Downers Grove, Ill.: InterVarsity Press, 1974), 36–38, 42–44.

19. John Henry Newman, *The Idea of a University: Defined and Illustrated in Nine Discourses Delivered to the Catholics of Dublin in Occasional Lectures and Essays Addressed to the Members of the Catholic University*, edited with an introduction and notes by Martin J. Svaglic (Notre Dame, Ind.: Univ. of Notre Dame Press, 1982), 103, 32–74. Some will recognize that insights much like Newman's on these points were extensively elaborated in the work of the Dutch philosopher Herman Dooyeweerd. The most accessible of Dooyeweerd's works is *In the Twilight of Western Thought: Studies in the Pretended Autonomy of Philosophical Thought* (Nutley, N.J.: Craig Press, 1960).

20. Philip Hefner, "Stories Science Tells: Defining the Human Quest," *Christian Century* (May 12, 1995): 508–13, quotations from 511 and 512.

21. Quentin Schultze, ed., *Dancing in the Dark: Youth, Popular Culture, and the Electronic Media*. (Grand Rapids: William B. Eerdmans, 1991).

22. Paul C. Vitz, *Psychology as Religion: The Cult of Self-Worship* (Berkeley: Univ. of California Press, 1985).

23. Robert Bellah et al., *Habits of the Heart: Individualism and Commitment in American Life* (Cambridge: Harvard Univ. Press, 1989).

CHAPTER FIVE

THE POSITIVE CONTRIBUTIONS

OF THEOLOGICAL CONTEXT

1. Theological perspectives may sometimes lead to a critique of technical methodologies. See, for instance, Mary Stewart Van Leeuwen's critique of some aspects of psychology in *The Sorcerer's Apprentice: A Christian Looks at the Changing Face of Psychology* (Downers Grove, Ill.: InterVarsity Press, 1982).

2. Peter L. Berger, *The Sacred Canopy: Elements of a Sociological Theory of Religion* (Garden City, N.Y.: Doubleday, 1969), 179–85.

3. John Milbank, *Theology and Social Theory: Beyond Secular Reason* (Oxford: Blackwell, 1990).

4. Probably the best known is John Rawls, *Theory of Justice* (Cambridge, Mass.: Belknap Press of Harvard Univ. Press, 1971).

5. One example of this approach is Richard J. Mouw, *The God Who Commands* (Notre Dame, Ind.: Univ. of Notre Dame Press, 1990). Christian thinkers have made many contributions to the field of ethics. Some of the better-known recent Protestant varieties are found in the works of Paul Ramsey, Stanley Hauerwas, and John Howard Yoder.

6. Carolyn Fluehr-Lobban, "Cultural Relativism and Universal Rights," *Chronicle of Higher Education* (June 9, 1995): B1–B2.

7. Barbara Johnson, ed., *Freedom and Interpretation: The Oxford Amnesty Lectures 1992* (New York: Basic Books, 1993). Quotations from editor's introduction 2, 6–7, and from Wayne C. Booth, "Individualism and the Mystery of the Social Self; or Does Amnesty Have a Leg to Stand On?," 101.

8. I realize, of course, that there are many attempts to construct such a naturalistic morality, and that relativism may foster tolerance and even some egalitarianism. No naturalistic theory, however, has a convincing principle with which to dissuade humans from their natural self-interest. The sort of Christian critique I have in mind is exemplified by Dennis O'Brien's comment in a review of Robert Wright, *The Moral Animal: Why We Are the Way We Are: The New Science of Evolutionary Psychology*, in *Commonweal*, June 2, 1995, p. 26. O'Brien observes: "But the notion that this brand of 'determinism' is the key to compassion is perverse. The best that can emerge from

thoroughgoing determinism would be a 'morality' of excuses (victims are blameless) never a morality (you have a moral responsibility not to blame victims!). I do not see how there can be a moral compulsion to forgive the victim, when there is no moral agent to whom one can appeal."

9. I am here dependent on the work of my philosopher friends, especially Alvin Plantinga and Nicholas Wolterstorff. Their views that I am best acquainted with are found in their edited volume, *Faith and Rationality: Reason and Belief in God* (Notre Dame: Univ. of Notre Dame Press, 1983), and Wolterstorff, *Reason Within the Bounds of Religion* (1976; Grand Rapids: William B. Eerdmans, 1984). Plantinga's recent works on the subject include *Warrant and Proper Function* (New York: Oxford Univ. Press, 1993) and *Warrant: The Current Debate* (New York: Oxford Univ. Press, 1993). Also important along the same lines are the recent works of William P. Alston, *Epistemic Justification: Essays in the Theory of Knowledge* (Ithaca: Cornell Univ. Press, 1989), *Faith, Reason, and Skepticism* (Philadelphia: Temple Univ. Press, 1992), and *Perceiving God: The Epistemology of Religious Experience* (Ithaca: Cornell Univ. Press, 1991).

10. Diogenes Allen, "Christianity and the Creed of Postmodernism," *Christian Scholars Review* 23:2 (Dec. 1993): 121.

11. Roger Lundin, *The Culture of Interpretation: Christian Faith and the Postmodern World* (Grand Rapids: William B. Eerdmans, 1993), passim and 259, 263, quoting from W. H. Auden, *Collected Poems,* ed. Edward Mendelson (New York: Random House, 1976), 311, 339–40.

12. Peter Berger, a Christian scholar himself, has worked hard to get around the implications of the stronger term "methodological atheism" which he popularized and which accurately describes the common expectation. See especially, *A Rumor of Angels: Modern Society and the Rediscovery of the Supernatural* (Garden City, N.Y.: Doubleday, 1970). The reason I prefer "methodological secularization" is that it does not imply an absence of God, since God has an intimate relationship to the secular (or the world). It just means that for the moment we will be keeping that dimension in the background.

13. For examples of Christian, although not always explicitly incarnational, approaches to these subjects, see the following volumes co-authored by various Fellows at the Calvin Center for Christian Scholarship: Peter De Vos, Calvin De Witt, Eugene Dykema, Vernon Ehlers, and Loren Wilkinson, *Earthkeeping in the '90s* (Grand Rapids: William B. Eerdmans, 1991); Clifford Christians, Eugene Dykema, Arie Leegwater, Stephen Monsma, Egbert Schuurman, and Lambert Van Poolen, *Responsible Technology: A Christian Perspective* (Grand Rapids: William B. Eerdmans, 1986); and Hessel Bouma III, Douglas Diekema, Edward Langerak, Theodore Rottman, and Allen Verhey, *Christian Faith, Health, & Medical Practice* (Grand Rapids: William B. Eerdmans, 1989).

14. From Gerard Manley Hopkins, "God's Grandeur," quoted from Louis Unter-meyer, ed., *Modern British Poetry: Mid-Century Edition* (New York: Harcourt, Brace, 1950), 42.

15. Richard F. Lovelace, *Dynamics of Spiritual Life: An Evangelical Theology of Renewal* (Downers Grove, Ill.: InterVarsity Press, 1979), 256. That volume and Lovelace's *The American Pietism of Cotton Mather: Origins of American Evangelicalism* (Grand Rapids: Christian Univ. Press, 1979) are fine examples of theologically informed historical scholarship. The former is addressed primarily to Christian audiences and the latter to the general scholarly community.

16. This section is a paraphrase of observations made in the afterword of Marsden, *Fundamentalism and American Culture: The Shaping of Twentieth-Century Evangelicalism, 1870–1925* (New York: Oxford Univ. Press, 1980), 229–30.

17. Stephen Hawking, *A Brief History of Time: From the Big Bang to Black Holes* (New York: Bantam Books, 1988), 175. Phillip E. Johnson, *Reason in the Balance: The Case Against Naturalism in Science, Law and Education* (Downers Grove, Ill.: InterVarsity Press, 1995), offers some telling critiques of this kind of thinking.

18. A fine selection of Niebuhr's writings is found in Robert McAfee Brown, ed., *The Essential Reinhold Niebuhr: Selected Essays and Addresses* (New Haven: Yale Univ. Press, 1986).

19. Graham Walker, *Moral Foundations of Constitutional Thought: Current Problems, Augustinian Prospects* (Princeton: Princeton Univ. Press, 1990), 4. Another insightful critique of current political outlooks is Glenn Tinder, *The Political Meaning of Christianity: An Interpretation* (Baton Rouge: Louisiana State Univ. Press, 1989). Also Jean Bethke Elshtain, *Augustine and the Limits of Politics* (Notre Dame, Ind.: Univ. of Notre Dame Press, 1996).

20. James W. Skillen in *Recharging the American Experiment: Principled Pluralism for Genuine Civic Community* (Grand Rapids: Baker Books, 1994).

Columnist William Raspberry cites the Center for Public Justice approvingly for its ability to address political and social problems in ways that cut across current party lines. Raspberry is particularly enthusiastic about the observations in a number of papers in a 1994 conference that the problems of the underclass in America need to be addressed not only as economic, political, and social problems, but also as a spiritual crisis as well. "Spiritually Transforming the Underclass," *Detroit News,* June 14, 1994, p. 11A.

## CHAPTER SIX
### BUILDING ACADEMIC COMMUNITIES

1. As discussed in Chapter Three, loyalties to such sub-communities need not conflict with good citizenship in the existing academic communities of disciplines, departments, and universities any more than loyalty to religious organizations conflicts with good citizenship with respect to the state.

2. For a brief account, see Kenneth Konyndyk, "Christianity Reenters Philosophi-

cal Circles," *Religious and Theological Studies Bulletin* 9 (Nov./Dec. 1995): 10–12 (origi-nally published in *Perspectives: A Journal of Reformed Thought,* Nov. 1992).

3. On American Catholic higher education, see Philip Gleason, *Contending with Modernity: Catholic Higher Education in the Twentieth Century* (New York: Oxford Univ. Press, 1995).

4. See, for instance, Theodore M. Hesburgh, C.S.C., ed, *The Challenge and Promise of a Catholic University* (Notre Dame, Ind.: Univ. of Notre Dame Press, 1994), and David J. O'Brien, *From the Heart of the American Church: Catholic Higher Education and American Culture* (Maryknoll, N.Y.: Orbis Books, 1994).

5. Allen Fisher, "Religious and Moral Education at Three Kinds of Liberal Arts Colleges: A Comparison of Curricula in Presbyterian, Evangelical, and Religiously Unaffiliated Liberal Arts Colleges," *Religious Education* 90:1 (Winter 1995): 30–49.

6. O'Brien, *From the Heart of the American Church,* 159–66, describes these and some other programs. At the end of 1995 the Lilly Fellows Program included a network of forty-seven church-related institutions and was adding six per year.

7. The Pew Younger Scholars Program, which provides graduate fellowships for graduates of evangelical Protestant colleges and summer seminars for prospective grad-uate students, is an excellent model for developing Christian academic leadership for the future. Similar programs are needed for other religious traditions.

8. Mark R. Schwehn, *Exiles from Eden: Religion and the Academic Vocation in America* (New York: Oxford Univ. Press, 1993), provides valuable analysis of this and related themes.

9. Galatians 5:22.


GETTING SPECIFIC: A READABLE APPENDIX

1. There is a large modern literature on the relationship between Christianity and history. See, for instance, the impressive collection in C. T. McIntire, ed., *God, History and Historians: An Anthology of Modern Views of History* (New York: Oxford Univ. Press, 1977). See also C. T. McIntire and Ronald A. Wells, eds., *History and Historical Understanding* (Grand Rapids: William B. Eerdmans, 1984), and especially the biblio-graphic essay by M. Howard Rienstra in George Marsden and Frank Roberts, eds., *A Christian View of History?* (Grand Rapids: William B. Eerdmans, 1975).

The series of edited volumes sponsored by the Institute for the Study of American Evangelicalism (ISAE) provide many examples of faith-informed historical study of a particular tradition. The volumes may be found among the edited works of Edith Blumhofer, Joel Carpenter, D. G. Hart, Nathan Hatch, George Marsden, Mark Noll, George Rawlyk, and Harry Stout. For a sampling of the work of ISAE authors, see D. G. Hart, ed, *Reckoning with the Past: Historical Essays on American Evangelicalism from the Institute for the Study of American Evangelicals* (Grand Rapids: Baker Books, 1995).

Ronald A. Wells, ed., *The Wars of America: Christian Views* (1981; Macon, Ga.: Mercer Univ. Press, 1991), offers a variety of Christian approaches to specific events.

2. Not all the works of all these authors illustrate the point, especially since some were converts to Christianity later in their careers. For a bibliography of Wolterstorff's works, see the first note of the introduction to this book.

3. Although I am working in a Catholic environment that I find congenial for the current enterprise, and while I can think of the works of a number of colleagues and others whose works could serve as illustrations, I do not feel competent to compile a list of examples of Catholic scholarship. However, if one peruses the publications of a Catholic press, such as the University of Notre Dame Press, or if one compiled a bibliography of the Catholic contributors to Theodore M. Hesburgh, C.S.C., ed, *The Challenge and Promise of a Catholic University* (Notre Dame, Ind.: Univ. of Notre Dame Press, 1994), one could clearly find Catholic counterparts to all the Protestant examples in this essay. Nevertheless, such recent scholarship is more limited than one might hope, given the resources of the Catholic Church and of Catholic universities and colleges.

As mentioned in the previous chapter, one should note also some revival of interest in faith-related scholarship among both Catholics and mainline Protestants as in *Collegium* (for Catholic scholars) and the Lilly Fellows Program in Humanities and the Arts, sponsored by the Lilly Endowment, Inc.

4. Mark A. Noll, *The Scandal of the Evangelical Mind* (Grand Rapids: William B. Eerdmans, 1994). Cf. also George Marsden, "The State of Evangelical Christian Scholarship," *Christian Scholar's Review* 17:4 (June 1988): 347–60. This essay was part of a symposium published in the same issue on "A New Agenda for Evangelical Thought." Other essays suggest agendas for Christians working in the sciences, economics, psychology, literature, and the arts.

5. Brian J. Walsh and J. Richard Middleton, *The Transforming Vision: Shaping a Christian World View* (Downers Grove, Ill.: InterVarsity Press, 1984), 203–14. James W. Sire, *Discipleship of the Mind: Learning to Love God in the Ways We Think* (Downers Grove, Ill.: InterVarsity Press, 1990), 219–43.

6. Also Harry Blamires, *The Christian Mind* (New York: Seabury Press, 1963), and Arthur F. Holmes, *Contours of a Worldview* (Grand Rapids: William B. Eerdmans, 1983).

7. David A. Fraser and Tony Campolo, *Sociology Through the Eyes of Faith* (1992), David G. Myers and Malcolm A. Jeeves, *Psychology Through the Eyes of Faith* (1987), Ronald A. Wells, *History Through the Eyes of Faith* (1989), Roger Lundin and Susan Gallagher, *Literature Through the Eyes of Faith* (1989), Harold M. Best, *Music Through the Eyes of Faith* (1993), Richard T. Wright, *Biology Through the Eyes of Faith* (1990), Richard C. Chewning, John W. Eby, and Shirley J. Roels, *Business Through the Eyes of Faith* (1990), Nicholas Wolterstorff, editor in chief, all published by HarperSanFrancisco.

8. Here are some examples from recent issues: Patrick A. Wilson, "Explaining a Finely Tuned Universe" (on the anthropic principle); Craig M. Gay, "When Evangelicals Take Capitalism Seriously"; Mark F. Williams, "Cosmic Katharsis, Creational

Norms, and the *Birds* of Aristophanes"; all from vol. 21:4 (June 1992). Mary Stewart Van Leeuwen, "Should Private Morality Go Public? A Christian Feminist Evaluation," 22:1 (Sept. 1992). Richard V. Pierard, "Civil Religiosity in a Marxist-Leninist Country: The Example of East Germany"; William Hasker, "Mr. Johnson for the Prosecution," review essay on Phillip E. Johnson, *Darwin on Trial* (Downers Grove, Ill.: InterVarsity Press, 1991); both from 22:2 (Dec. 1992). John P. Tiemstra, "Christianity and Economics: A Review of the Recent Literature"; Timothy A. Smith, "Bach and the Cross"; Phillip E. Johnson, "Response to Hasker"; William Hasker, "Reply to Johnson"; all from 22:3 (March 1993). Diogenes Allen, "The End of the Modern World"; Calvin Redekop, "Mennonites, Creation, and Work"; David Wilcox, "Covenantal Science: Impossible or Required?"; Howard J. Van Till, "Is Special Creation a Heresy?"; Larry A. Brown, "Ring Around the Collar: American Comedy and the Clergy"; all from 22:4 (June 1993). Diogenes Allen, "Christianity and the Creed of Postmodernism"; Craig M. Gay, "Christianity and the 'Homelessness' of the Modern Mind"; Richard J. Mouw, "Creational Politics: Some Calvinist Amendments"; David L. Wilcox, "Athens and the National Academy of Science: Is There No Philosophy of Science?"; all from 23:2 (Dec. 1993); "Theme Issue: Christianity and Bioethics" (a symposium on "Bioethics in a Post-Consensus Society" and seven articles), 23:3 (March, 1994); "Special Issue: Christianity and Economics" (6 articles), 24:2 (Dec. 1994). *Christian Scholar's Review* is sponsored by about forty Christian colleges and universities.

9. See Walsh and Middleton, "A Bibliography We Can't Live Without," in *Transforming Vision*, for journals in other fields.

10. Although technically a theological project, another of those funded by the Pew Evangelical Scholars the same year (1994) is that of Charles Robert Marsh, Jr., "Theologies in Crisis: Conflicting Images of God in the American Civil Rights Movement."

11. The following are the titles with authors in parentheses:

*Earthkeeping: Christian Stewardship of Natural Resources.* Grand Rapids: William B. Eerdmans, 1980. Revised as *Earthkeeping in the '90s.* Grand Rapids: William B. Eerdmans, 1991. (Peter De Vos, Calvin De Witt, Eugene Dykema, Vernon Ehlers, and Loren Wilkinson)

*Society, State, and Schools: A Case for Structural and Confessional Pluralism.* Grand Rapids: William B. Eerdmans, 1981. (Rockne McCarthy, Donald Oppewal, Walfred Peterson, and Gordon Spykman)

*The Sorcerer's Apprentice: A Christian Looks at the Changing Face of Psychology.* Downers Grove, Ill.: InterVarsity Press, 1982. (Mary Stewart Van Leeuwen)

*Faith and Rationality: Reason and Belief in God.* Univ. of Notre Dame Press, 1983. (William Alston, David Holwerda, George Marsden, George Mavrodes, Alvin Plantinga, and Nicholas Wolterstorff)

*Sociology and the Human Image.* Downers Grove, Ill.: InterVarsity Press, 1983. (David Lyon)

*The Responsibility of Hermeneutics.* Grand Rapids: William B. Eerdmans, 1985. (Roger Lundin, Anthony Thiselton, and Clarence Walhout)

*Karl Mannheim: The Development of His Thought.* New York: St. Martin Press, 1986. (Henk E. S. Woldring)

*Responsible Technology: A Christian Perspective.* Grand Rapids: William B. Eerdmans, 1986. (Clifford Christians, Eugene Dykema, Arie Leegwater, Stephen Monsma, Egbert Schuurman, and Lambert Van Poolen)

*Narrating Psychology or How Psychology Gets Made.* Bristol, Ind.: Wyndham Hall Press, 1987. (Mary Vander Goot)

*Science Held Hostage: What's Wrong with Creation Science and Evolutionism.* Downers Grove, Ill.: InterVarsity Press, 1988. (Clarence Menninga, Howard Van Till, and Davis Young)

*Reforming Economics: A Christian Perspective on Economic Theory and Practice.* Lewiston, N.Y.: Edwin Mellen, 1990. (W. Fred Graham, George Monsma, Jr., Carl Sinke, Alan Storkey, and John Tiemstra)

*Christian Faith, Health, & Medical Practice.* Grand Rapids: William B. Eerdmans, 1989. (Hessel Bouma III, Douglas Diekema, Edward Langerak, Theodore Rottman, and Allen Verhey)

*Let My People Live: Faith and Struggle in Central America.* Grand Rapids: William B. Eerdmans, 1988. (Guillermo Cook, Michael Dodson, Lance Grahn, Sidney Rooy, John Stam, and Gordon Spykman)

*Portraits of Creation: Biblical and Scientific Perspectives on the World's Formation.* Grand Rapids: William B. Eerdmans, 1990. (Robert Snow, John Stek, Howard Van Till, and Davis Young)

*Dancing in the Dark: Youth, Popular Culture and the Electronic Media.* Grand Rapids: William B. Eerdmans, 1991. (Roy Anker, James Bratt, William Romanowski, Quentin Schultze, John Worst, and Lambert Zuidervaart)

*After Eden: Facing the Challenge of Gender Reconciliation.* Grand Rapids: William B. Eerdmans, 1993. (Annelies Knoppers, Margaret Koch, Douglas Schuurman, Helen Sterk, and Mary Stewart Van Leeuwen)

*A Vision with a Task: Christian Schooling for Responsive Discipleship.* Grand Rapids: Baker Books, 1994. (Doug Blomberg, Peter DeBoer, Robert Koole, Gloria Goris Stronks, Harro Van Brummelen, and Steven Vryhof)

*Educating Christian Teachers for Responsive Discipleship.* Lanham, Md.: Univ. Press of America, 10′3. (Doug Blomberg, Peter DeBoer, Robert Koole, Gloria Goris Stronks, and Harro Van Brummelen)

*Coming of Age: Protestantism in Contemporary Latin America.* Lanham, Md.: Univ. Press of America, 1994. (Edited by Daniel Miller)

*Assessment in Christian Higher Education: Rhetoric and Reality.* Lanham, Md.: Univ. Press of America, 1994. (Edited by D. John Lee and Gloria Goris Stronks)

*Christian Political Activism at the Crossroads.* Lanham, Md.: Univ. Press of America, 1994. (Edited by William Stevenson, Jr.)

# Index

Abortion, 49
Academic freedom, 14, 36
African Americans, 34–35, 117; perspectives of, 52–54
Allen, Diogenes, 89
American Academy of Religion, 7, 124 n.13
American Association of University Professors, 123 n.2
American Civil Liberties Union, 38
American Scientific Affiliation, 102
American Society of Church History, 31
Amnesty International, 87
Anabaptists, 117
Anthropology, 86, 96, 116
Aquinas, Thomas, 115
The arts, 92
Auden, W. H., 90, 117–18
Augustine and Augustinian Christianity, 9, 44–45, 55, 97–100
Ayer, A. J., 27

Background religious commitments, 48–51
Baylor University, 109
Bellah, Robert, 79
Bender, Thomas, 51, 121 n.5, 127 n.5
Berger, Peter, 84, 132 n.12
Bible. *See* Scripture
Bibliography of Christian scholarship, 113–19 and *passim*
Biology, 114

Bloom, Allan, 103
*Books and Culture,* 115
Booth, Wayne C., 87
Boyer, Paul, 129 n.9
Bradley, James, 116
Buddhism, 10
Business, 114

Calvin Center for Christian Scholarship, 118
Calvin College, 42, 60–61, 72, 109
Campus ministries, 20
Carter, Stephen A., 20, 44, 105
Catholic University of Ireland, 76
Catholicism, 32, 48, 59–60, 76, 101–2, 103–4, 114, 135 n.3; mentioned, 17, 20, 21; prejudice against, 14, 15, 33, 37; social encyclicals, 128–29 n.4
Center for Public Justice, 99, 125 n.20
Chesterton, G. K., 47
Christian attitudes in scholarship, 54–55, 107–9
Christian Coalition, 34
Christian College Coalition, 114
Christian Colleges and Universities, 11, 103–7, 109–10, 128 n.3
Christian perspectives, 10–12 and *passim*; opposition to, 5–10; why not welcomed, 13–24. *See also* Religious perspectives
Christian right (political), 33–34, 38
*Christian Scholar's Review,* 114–15

# Index